PRAISE FOR *UNAPOLOGETIC*

"*Unapologetic* is a beautiful, insightful, and powerful analysis of this moment, Black movements, and Black radical futures. Both Charlene Carruthers's work as an organizer and organic intellectual and her writing in *Unapologetic* embody the Black radical tradition and the best of Black feminism today. Carruthers confronts the difficulties of organizing in this era, while also detailing the possibilities of collective struggle. She helps us understand the contours of a Black queer feminist future and what we all must do to get there. This is a must-read for anyone committed to freedom and liberation."

—Cathy J. Cohen, *Democracy Remixed: Black Youth and the Future of American Politics*

"*Unapologetic* is as much a narrative about collective youth-driven organizing by those affiliated with the current Movement for Black Lives as it is a story about how one young Black woman from the South Side of Chicago found herself leading one of the most consequential formations of the past decade. The book offers practical tips for organizers along with a critical analysis of the promise and pitfalls of this current iteration of the Black radical tradition. As an organizer, I found myself nodding along as I read this terrific book while taking notes to improve my own practice."

—Mariame Kaba, founder of Project NIA and cofounder of Survived & Punished

"Charlene Carruthers carries the burden, the beauty, the wisdom of four hundred years of Black struggle. But she also brings a critical perspective and a creative vision, rooted in her extensive experience as an organizer and organic intellectual, and in her fierce and fearless commitment to truth. This is an inspiring, powerful, but difficult book because she confronts our movements, our people, our closeted silences, toxic masculinity, patriarchal violence, romantic and selective historical memory, and our future head-on, through a radical Black queer feminist lens. Welcome to the Black radical tradition."

—Robin D. G. Kelley, author of *Freedom Dreams: The Black Radical Imagination*

"*Unapologetic* serves as our marching orders. Charlene gives us not just a manual but a prayer, an intention, a critical path forward, and a deep analysis on where we've been. She educates us about community violence and state violence, and provides the clarity to show why Black liberation is crucial for us all."

—Patrisse Khan-Cullors, coauthor of *When They Call You a Terrorist: A Black Lives Matter Memoir*

"Leadership is the ability to not only make your own way but to return to give others a road map that they, too, can follow. This is what Charlene Carruthers does with *Unapologetic*. She offers us a guide to getting free with incisive prose, years of grassroots organizing experience, and a deeply intersectional lens. She doesn't forget any of *us* and reminds us that bringing all of ourselves and our people with us is the only way any of us will get free."

—Janet Mock, author of *Redefining Realness and Surpassing Certainty*

"Charlene Carruthers is a powerful organizer, radical thinker, paradigm shifter, and one of the most influential political voices of her generation. Anyone seriously interested in the struggle for Black liberation in this country needs to listen carefully to what she has to say."

—Barbara Ransby, author of *Ella Baker and the Black Freedom Movement* and *Making All Black Lives Matter*

"With this clear call to action, Charlene Carruthers's *Unapologetic* is a desperately needed analysis of the past, the present, and where we must head into the future. It's a must-read for everyone who wants deeper, honest insight into the struggles happening in our country right now, clarifying why stopping anti-Black racism, homophobia, and sexism and building transformative power intersectionally are urgent necessities for our families, our communities, and the nation."

—Kristin Rowe-Finkbeiner, author, executive director, and cofounder of MomsRising.org

"Charlene Carruthers speaks with the authenticity and authority of an organizer from the front lines of struggle. Cut from the cloth of the South Side of Chicago, Carruthers offers a critical perspective into the experience of organizing and building a movement from the inside. As an organizer, Charlene provides rare insight into the strategies, tactics, and raging debates that animate the phenomenon of Black Lives Matter. If you want to understand this movement and the people whose hands are dirty from working with the grassroots, then you need this book."

—Keeanga-Yamahtta Taylor, author of *From #BlackLivesMatter to Black Liberation*

"This brilliant and powerful book is a clarion call to keep alive the Black radical tradition in these reactionary times. Charlene A. Carruthers is an exemplary organic intellectual rooted in the struggles of black poor and working people, especially LGBTQ youth, with a subtle analysis and an international vision for freedom. She stands in the great lineage of Harriet Tubman, Ida B. Wells-Barnett, and Marsha P. Johnson—grand fighters and great lovers of everyday black people and oppressed folk everywhere!"

—Dr. Cornel West

UNAPOLOGETIC

UNAPOLOGETIC

A BLACK, QUEER, AND FEMINIST MANDATE FOR RADICAL MOVEMENTS

CHARLENE A. CARRUTHERS

BEACON PRESS
BOSTON

BEACON PRESS
Boston, Massachusetts
www.beacon.org

Beacon Press books
are published under the auspices of
the Unitarian Universalist Association of Congregations.

22 21 20   8 7 6 5 4 3

This book is printed on acid-free paper that meets the uncoated paper
ANSI/NISO specifications for permanence as revised in 1992.

Text design and composition by Kim Arney

"Paul Robeson" reprinted by consent of Brooks Permissions. Brief quote
from p. 414 from *Black Boy* by Richard Wright, copyright 1937, 1942,
1944, 1945 by Richard Wright; renewed © 1973 by Ellen Wright.
Reprinted by permission of HarperCollins Publishers.

Library of Congress Cataloging-in-Publication Data

Names: Carruthers, Charlene A., author.
Title: Unapologetic : a Black, queer, and feminist mandate for our movement /
    Charlene A. Carruthers.
Description: Boston : Beacon Press, [2018] | Includes bibliographical
    references and index.
Identifiers: LCCN 2017058987 (print) | LCCN 2018024924 (ebook) |
    ISBN 9780807019429 (e-book) | ISBN 9780807039823 (paperback)
Subjects: LCSH: African American lesbians—Political activity—United
    States—21st century. | African American women—Political activity—United
    States—21st century. | Feminism—United States—21st century. | Black
    power—United States. | Black lives matter movement—United States. |
    African Americans—Civil rights.
Classification: LCC HQ75.6.U5 (ebook) | LCC HQ75.6.U5 C36 2018 (print) |
    DDC 305.48/896073—dc23
LC record available at https://lccn.loc.gov/2017058987

For my mother; my father; my brother and sister and niece; Harriet Tubman, whose gun is at my back; my grandparents who migrated north; the members of BYP100; Mary Hooks and the mandate; my ancestors, elders, and comrades. This book is possible because of you. Thank you for being my North Star.

CONTENTS

AUTHOR'S NOTE

Unapologetic is a book for all people who are curious about and committed to the struggle for Black liberation. There are at least two ways that you can read this book. The first is to read it to build, sharpen, or deepen your analysis or understanding of core concepts and practices to use in building social justice movements for collective liberation. While there are many types of analysis one can use, this book is based in Black radical, feminist, queer, and anti-capitalist theories and practices. The ideas I share are the result of rigorous reading, film watching, conversations with comrades, family members, and neighbors, and movement-building experiences on the ground. I encourage all readers to use this book to engage in principled struggle through direct communication and honest dialogue.

You can also read this book for a historical account of the Black radical tradition that centers the stories and movements led by people who are not typically lauded. There are stories throughout this book that should be explored more deeply and subjects warranting books of their own. My intention is to share stories you may not have heard before and offer perspectives on strategies Black folks have used for centuries.

Unapologetic includes a number of complex ideas and terms that I attempt to make clear through stories and practical examples. I do not expect all readers to understand all of the concepts equally. Don't be afraid to use a dictionary. I use one when I read too. Below, defined concisely, are some key terms I use in this book.

Anti-Blackness: a system of beliefs and practices that destroy, erode, and dictate the humanity of Black people.

Abolition: as defined by Critical Resistance, a long-term political vision with the goal of eliminating imprisonment, policing, and surveillance and creating lasting alternatives to punishment and imprisonment.

Black radical tradition: a collection of cultural, intellectual, action-oriented labor aimed at disrupting social, political, economic, and cultural norms originating in anticolonial and antislavery efforts.

Capitalism: an economic system in which the means of production, access to goods, and the value of goods are controlled by private individuals and corporations. *Racial capitalism*, as theorized by Cedric Robinson, argues that this system was built and flourished through the exploitation of people through slavery, imperialism, and genocide. *Neoliberalism* is a model of capitalism that operates through the privatization of public goods, deregulation of trade, diminishment of social services, and emphasis on individual freedoms.

Feminism: in the view of bell hooks, a movement to end sexism, sexist exploitation, and oppression. This includes political, social, and ideological methods and work.

LGBTQ: the acronym commonly used as an umbrella term for lesbian, gay, bisexual, transgender, and questioning (or queer) people and communities. I use the term interchangeably with "queer" throughout the book. "Queer" generally means outside the norm or deviant. The use of the term "femme" throughout the book refers to a gender identity that is taken up in various ways throughout the queer and trans community by people who may not identify as women and do identify as feminine. My use of the term is in the context of campaigns and does not refer to "femme" as used by lesbian and queer women. All of these terms will continue to evolve.

Radical Black feminisms are rooted in the lived experiences and interlocking oppressions of Black people on the basis of race, class, and gender and aim to dismantle all forms of systemic oppression. I rely heavily on radical US Black feminisms throughout the text, but there are many other forms across the diaspora.

Reparations: as defined by the National Coalition of Blacks for Reparations in America, are political demands and projects that entail repairing, healing, and restoring a people injured by governments or corporations because of their group identity and in violation of their fundamental human rights. In addition to being a matter of justice, it is a principle of international human rights.

Transformative justice: as defined by Generation Five, is a liberatory approach to violence that seeks safety and accountability without relying on alienation, punishment, or state or systemic violence, including incarceration or policing.

———

Though *Unapologetic* reflects insights gained on my journey thus far as an activist, community organizer, and leader, it is not a comprehensive history of my community organizing experiences, BYP100, or my personal life. The book about the history of BYP100 has yet to be written, and it's not time for me to write a memoir about my life and organizing. My intent is to balance stories of my community-organizing experiences, BYP100, and my personal life in order to inspire revolutionary action. This book is an invitation and guide, not a final plan.

PREFACE

Unapologetic is an offering to our ancestors, my family, our movement, and the generations who will hold the struggle for Black liberation to come. I began writing this book over five years ago as a personal exploration of freedom, liberation, and movement building. Much like my life in general, where I landed in the book is both far away from and close to where I began. I was born and raised on the South Side of Chicago to parents whose own parents migrated from the Deep South. Their ways of talking, eating, and dealing with life still live in my body and in the choices I make.

I left home at eighteen and spent nearly ten years exploring the United States and the world. As much as Chicago made me, the world has raised me. Whether my work took me to Murfreesboro, Tennessee, to door-knock and gain support for comprehensive health-care reform or to Haiti to learn how to support nation-building efforts, I learned that change was not only possible, it was inevitable. I also learned that the change needed for my people has only come because we insisted on it. Frederick Douglass famously observed that "power concedes nothing without a demand." I believe that we must go further and say that power concedes nothing without an *organized* demand.

Growing up in Chicago taught me about power even before I could define what it meant for my mother, my family, and myself as a little Black girl. My earliest memories about power come from the visits I took with my mother to the public aid office. I remember walking into a nondescript brown building on Root Street where we would enter a room full of Black and Brown women. Most of the women had children with them and, like my mother, were there to secure food stamps or cash to support their families. The room was colorful and always noisy. We would walk up to the front desk, which was placed on high, and even then the symbolism of this was evident to me, and I found the arrangement uncomfortable and odd. I also didn't understand why we had to wait in a room all day for a conversation of no more than fifteen minutes with a caseworker. I didn't understand why the caseworker asked my mother invasive questions about my very present father. I didn't know the government viewed Black fathers as a barrier to need and Black mothers as unworthy of dignified treatment.

Those childhood visits to the welfare office with its fluorescent lights, along with experiences of growing up in Back of the Yards, Woodlawn, and Gage Park, stuck inside me as I began to learn about community organizing. But it was a visit to South Africa at the age of eighteen that blew my mind and was a watershed moment. As a young Black woman from the racially segregated city of Chicago, I had little understanding of what apartheid meant in a global sense. But unlike the hours of documentaries I watched about the US civil rights and Black Power movements as a child, that experience affected me viscerally and sparked my commitment to improving the conditions of oppressed people worldwide.

Reflecting back, in college, where I should have been exposed to books and materials about the Black radical tradition, I didn't have the language I now have to understand oppression based on race, class, and gender identity. I didn't have the words to explain why Black students had access to vastly different educational environments depending on their zip code. I surely did not understand why Blackness was most often talked about in the media as monolithic, why identities and experiences that most closely fit the dominant culture were praised, and why anyone on the margins of gender and sexuality was criminalized, degraded, or rendered invisible.

Under the guidance of Dr. Venus Evans Winters, I read sociological texts that matched my personal experiences of racism, housing segregation, and policing that helped bring global anti-Blackness, patriarchy, and capitalism into focus so I could fit the pieces together. History courses exposed me to the role of the "race women" who, at the turn of the century, practiced Black activism in the South after the disenfranchisement of Black men. I was hooked on racial justice and started to understand the expansive nature of Blackness and what it meant worldwide.

People in social justice movements taught me to think more expansively about Black freedom and collective liberation. Sitting at the feet of reproductive justice leaders, queer and transgender leaders, and elders and hearing their stories taught me what I didn't learn as a college student. Being in movement work taught me how to take information, put it into context, and produce my own knowledge to understand current conditions and to create a vision for the future. Movement work put the histories of Black feminist and LGBTQ movements on my radar. In political education sessions, I learned about anti-Blackness.

Unapologetic is based on centuries of such information and context created by people committed to collective liberation. Black abolitionists, race women and men, nationalists, communists, socialists, feminists, theologians, and queer and transgender liberationists have built the foundation for what must be done today. Our movement taught me the value of study, rigorous thinking, and discipline to take action. Thanks to the movement, I know what actions are necessary and why we must take action. The movement taught me that work for justice has always been done and that my generation has a responsibility to carry the struggle for liberation forward. And the movement taught me the necessity of showing up for all oppressed people.

I am one of many who have taken up that responsibility in my generation. Since 2013, I have steered the growth and development of BYP100 (Black Youth Project 100), one of the most prolific and integral Black liberation movement organizations of the twenty-first century. Our team is full of brilliant liberationists who believe that a Black freedom movement is possible in our lifetime and that it must be Black, queer, and feminist. Following the vision of BYP100 leader Fresco Steez, we made it cool and relevant to be "unapologetically Black." It was not popular to build an all-Black activist organization or common for a membership-based organization such as ours to be led by young, Black women and LGBTQ folks, but we did it anyway.

We intended that the organization's chapters be its lifeblood, but even with our best efforts, we didn't always get it right. As the sole staff member during the first year, I also helped build the Chicago chapter from the ground alongside Jasson Perez, Rose Afriyie, Asha Ransby-Sporn, Janae Bonsu, and Johnae Strong, who soon expanded their roles to become national leaders in the organization. As BYP100 developed, our roles grew and lines blurred. My efforts were split—with half in Chicago and the other half in the national organization. Sometimes it felt I couldn't do justice to either effort, and sometimes I longed to focus on local organizing. Still, I recognized that much of our strength came from the varying perspectives and landscapes throughout the country. So, when I was not developing the Chicago chapter leadership, I traveled to support the building of chapters in New York City, Philadelphia, the San Francisco Bay Area, and Washington, DC. With little money at the beginning, I often slept on couches. I wasn't a typical executive director in that I did at least as much work building chapters as I did fund-raising and doing media work. It was hard to know if I always made the right call in how I spent my time, but I believe that our influence will continue to be felt for years to come. BYP100 is a part of our generation's vanguard, and I feel blessed by our ancestors to be among its leaders.

In today's struggle for Black liberation, I have been a witness to grave injustices against our people. Because we are not yet free, I continue to put my body on the line in Black-led uprisings and rebellions across the United States of a scale not seen since the 1960s and 1970s. Because of my experiences and what I know of history, I carry the knowledge and traumas of Black insurgency into the twenty-first century.

My journey has been mentally, physically, emotionally, and spiritually challenging. I've doubted my leadership and abilities on several occasions. When it would have been easy to boast, I remained quiet and worked. Where it would have been easy to fire back publicly against character attacks, I shared my anger and remorse with a circle of trusted comrades who are now family. Since then, though, I've learned that grace is an insufficient response to injustice. In the past, on occasion, I have been afraid to speak for fear of being too aggressive and taking up too much space. *Unapologetic* is a public declaration that I am no longer afraid to say what must be said and that our movement has a mandate that will not be silenced or disappeared.

Unapologetic exists at the crossroads of retrospection and vision. It is a testament to my own and our collective past and present, as well as a look to the future. It is a work of history, theory, practice, and vision. Use it to help expand your understanding of the Black radical tradition. Use its examples of community organizing and intellectual labor to answer old questions and ask new ones. For me, completing this book was a risk worth taking. I wanted to bear witness and to state clearly a mandate for what must be done in our movement today. *Unapologetic* contains histories that help tell a more complete story of the Black radical tradition. It is also a call for commitment, a call for action, a call for us all to be transformed, dismantling what doesn't serve our collective work, and for contemporary examples that illuminate how this generation of Black activists is carrying forth the Black radical tradition.

I don't expect my work to end here, with these pages. Whether your work begins or continues after digesting this, my greatest hope is that of any good organizer. I hope it shakes you, agitates you, and leaves you uncomfortable enough to take revolutionary action for the sake of our collective liberation. If I succeed in that, then I'll be deeply grateful and consider this labor of love and commitment a job well done.

CHAPTER I

ALL OF US OR NONE OF US

This focusing upon our own oppression is embodied in the concept of identity politics. We believe that the most profound and potentially most radical politics come directly out of our own identity. . . . If Black women were free, it would mean that everyone else would have to be free since our freedom would necessitate the destruction of all the systems of oppression.

—COMBAHEE RIVER COLLECTIVE, 1977

Nothing brings out the true colors of people in the United States as effectively or honestly as a presidential election. The best and worst of humanity have a way of showing themselves in a never-ending cycle. Of course, we know that candidates will say and do almost anything to win. We also know that every four years Democrats and Republicans raise astronomical amounts of money to spend on consultants, ads, field operations, hats, yard signs, data analysis, direct voter outreach, and a host of other things. Candidates visit churches, host rallies, kiss babies, and eat fried chicken, which they hope demonstrates that they understand what people care about. And though this performance helps them raise money, it is all ultimately to win on Election Day.

Campaign strategists make choices about which groups will amass the most money and best serve their interests and consider which messages will resonate most. The 2016 presidential election campaigns were a prime example of how the messages matter. Unsurprisingly, just what groups were targeted and the message they received are at the center of the debate of why Hillary Clinton—whose party, campaign committee, and supporting Super PACs raised about $1.2 billion dollars—lost the election to an opponent, Republican Donald Trump, with less money, multiple accusations of sexual assault, and no experience as an elected official or public servant.[1]

Regardless of what news media you read and watched, the chatter predicted a Clinton victory. Polling-data darling Nate Silver predicted that Clinton would win in a landslide. She was pro-choice and backed by a host of major feminist organizations, labor unions, and mainstream progressive organizations. White women were an assumed constituency. First Lady Michelle Obama even hit the campaign trail to support Clinton, while President Barack Obama ventured that it would be a "personal insult" if Black voters did not turn out and vote for Clinton. As we now know, she won the Black vote and the popular vote—and lost in the Electoral College.

I was among those who were fooled into believing that this country would never elect a racist billionaire who had multiple accusations of rape and no experience as a public servant. Many comrades and I were readying ourselves to finally take up a real fight with the Democratic Party with the Obama administration leaving. When I woke at 2:30 a.m. to learn that Clinton had lost the election, I was not alone in my shock or my profound lack of understanding of what had happened. Everyone—pundits, progressives, and countless ordinary people—sought to understand who and what was to blame for Clinton's loss.

Unsurprisingly, what surfaced was typical of the so-called American Left. In no more than two days after the election, the "failure of identity politics" articles started to roll out. Identity politics entail stances and actions based on people's identification along lines of race, gender, class, religion, disability, and other lived experiences. Oddly (but intentionally) enough, the identities these articles targeted as being divisive matched up well with the groups Trump's campaign targeted: women, Muslims, and Black and Brown people.

Former believers in the positive possibilities of identity politics—like John B. Judis, author of *The Emerging Democratic Majority*, who once exalted the potential for "professionals, women and minorities" to create Democratic majorities—now wrote scathing indictments, changing their minds overnight. As to why the Democrats failed, Judis concluded that "they overestimated the strength of a coalition based on identity politics."[2]

Political scientist Mark Lilla called for the complete elimination of identity politics in liberalism. He claimed that there was a "moral panic about racial, gender and sexual identity that has distorted liberalism's message and prevented it from becoming a unifying force capable of governing."[3]

This call for the end of identity politics illuminates the need to end liberalism. When liberals say we need change in moderation, I hear "not you" and "not yet." When pale and male scholars argue that "Democrats can't win elections simply by appealing to the identity groups of the rising American electorate" (as Judis wrote), I hear a poor and inaccurate analysis of how the Democratic Party operates.[4] There was no single Democratic Party strategy to invest in women and Black and Brown communities in the 2016 election campaign. Black women, one of the party's most loyal constituencies, are consistently undervalued and under-resourced as candidates.

These calls to end identity politics emerged in a moment of shock felt around the world. But what they failed to fully acknowledge is how whiteness, maleness, and working-class and upper-class status—all identities—played major roles in the election's outcome. Additionally, the targeting of women, Blacks, and Latinx people as poor political investments demonstrates dishonesty and lack of rigor in explaining Clinton's defeat. Clinton was defeated partly because the media, progressive organizations, and Democratic Party leaders underestimated the power of sexism, white anxiety, fear-mongering, and voter suppression that kept many marginalized people (e.g., formerly incarcerated and those without government ID) from the polls. Although some people predicted the defeat, there was a vast miscalculation of support for Trump, and likewise the effectiveness and attractiveness of the Democratic Party were overrated throughout the campaign. The election delivered insight into the real unmasked feelings of the progressives and liberals who showed not even a modicum of solidarity with oppressed people. The liberal "Left" sentiments I've read and heard are not markedly different from those of the Trump supporters they admonish.

Changing this dynamic would require restructuring power in the Democratic National Committee, all affiliated party institutions, and the progressive philanthropic community. A true shift in US politics would require white liberal and progressive women to pull the wool from over their eyes and accept that white women consistently vote against the interests of women's rights by supporting anti-choice, classist, racist, and sexist candidates. As I previously argued, power concedes nothing without an organized demand. Whether that demand is organized before the 2020 elections is yet to be determined.

Identity politics in the United States are as old as the nation's founding. Back then, white men with varying levels of wealth and access to resources debated and made choices to protect the interests of the ruling, slaveholding, and landowning class. The identity politics of white Christian men in the Ku Klux Klan—from its founding in 1865 through its many resurgences—have meant rape and murder of Black people. The most powerful in this country, including those who control public school curricula, the media, and government, used their common identity to encourage collective amnesia and distort perception of what truly makes up the fabric of this country.

But identity politics are not inherently or necessarily divisive. It can be easy to forget this, but it's people and the oppressive systems they uphold that create social divisions. Despite the durability of oppressive systems and the stories that help to uphold them, there is another way. It is when identity politics move from the margins that liberation becomes possible. The Combahee River Collective, a Black feminist grassroots organization founded in 1974 and led by Black women (including Black lesbians), authored a manifesto and led campaigns in which they not only articulated liberatory identity politics but also practiced them.[5] Truly transformative identity politics come from the feminist and queer streams within the Black radical tradition. The promise of collective liberation and its power exists in their overlap and even in their divergence.

BLACK, QUEER, AND FEMINIST POSSIBILITIES

I'm never more targeted by hatred from within the Black movement community than I am when our work is highly visible. I've been called out for being a dangerous lesbian and someone parents should keep away from their children. Feminism and queer politics (and the people who engage in them) are often slandered and called divisive. This is nothing new. Barbara Smith's "Toward a Black Feminist Criticism" essay, written in 1977, aired a deep and righteous frustration about the invisibility of Black feminist writers in all areas of culture and society. She understood the publishing of this essay as dangerous but necessary in a time when a movement advancing Black feminism was desperately needed. Writing as Black women, lesbians, and feminists means contending with violence that no one should have to deal with.

Verbal and physical attacks on Black lesbian feminists may seem surprising to some, as if they belong to a less enlightened era, but they are predictable in times of our high activity and visibility. Regardless of the risk, however, we Black queer and trans women have been on the front lines of anti-police and Black liberation organizing in the United States. We have been there after Black men and boys have been slain by police officers and vigilantes. We have shown up, even when masses have not, after a Black woman, girl, or trans, or queer, or gender-nonconforming person has been killed. And we will continue to show up. What we choose to support and oppose defines our politics.

Black feminists have coined terms in theorizing about the multiplicity of our experiences and expertise: "double jeopardy," "triple oppressions," "interlocking oppressions," and "intersectionality." No one experiences the world through a single identity. Understanding and expressing what it means when one's race, class, gender, and sexuality simultaneously shape one's political values is part of a long tradition of being a Black woman who is queer or transgender or both. While the language has evolved over the years (from the likes of "Negro" and "transsexual"), the conditions and systems of oppression have been consistently violent.

Today's movements are fortunate to have ready access to books, poetry, films, and social media to help make sense of what liberation requires. Decades of intellectual labor and community organizing have created the stories and understandings we have today about living at the intersections of race, class, gender, and sexuality. Unfortunately, far too many of us take this for granted, as we take for granted Black radical lesbian Audre Lorde's wise declaration that "there is no thing as a single-issue struggle because we do not live single-issue lives." Our luminaries deserve more than to be distilled into pithy quotes. Their intellectual labor should be used to guide our strategies to build movements.

Historically the Black radical tradition has related to the freedom struggles of other oppressed peoples worldwide and built itself alongside them. Feminist and Pan-Africanist leader Amy Jacques Garvey, editor of the women's page in the *Negro World*, the weekly newspaper of the United Negro Improvement Association (UNIA), wrote extensively about the need to be anti-capitalist and anti-imperialist and about the interlocking oppressions due to race, class, and gender. Founded by Jamaican-born Marcus Garvey and his first wife, Amy Ashwood Garvey, the UNIA had over six million members at its height, more Black people than were members of any other organization of their time or ours. There were conflicting ideas about women's capabilities and role in the UNIA, but the organization was a place where Black women could and did develop as political leaders.[6]

The resilience evident after decades of Black, queer, feminist organizing proves that identity politics can expand our paths to collective liberation. There are countless examples of what happens when marginalized people take up big structural issues: all people can benefit. For example, the Black Panther Party Free Breakfast Program and the ongoing Fight for $15 campaign for a living wage set out to improve conditions for all people.

Black feminists and LGBTQ activists are labeled "hijackers" and said to be divisive or co-opting or distracting from what is important, and what is "important" is the mainstream narrative propped up by patriarchy and misogyny (straight-up hatred of women). In the popular stories of social movements in the United States and the broader African diaspora, the Black feminist and queer liberation movements, which intersect and diverge, are often rendered invisible.

Identity doesn't dictate behavior or values. We learn values and choose political commitments. Just because a person is Black, a woman, and queer or transgender (or both) does not mean one is automatically radical or a revolutionary. Being radical is a choice, and it takes work. A person with a marginalized identity can engage in conservative, oppressive political work, and activists, organizers, and intellectuals living under capitalism, colonialism, anti-Black racism, and patriarchy require years of unlearning or decolonization. Our customs, beliefs, values, behaviors, and even our bodies are shaped by the societies and powerful systems we grow up in. At best, as marginalized people, we choose to resist. At worst, we internalize oppression and live in ways that do not serve our collective liberation.

THE BLACK QUEER FEMINIST LENS

It might be surprising to read that I believe it is normal to be prejudiced, racist, homophobic, transphobic, classist, and ableist in this country. I believe this because in the United States—and arguably across the world—values-based institutions that a majority of people engage with, including schools—usually support a status quo in which what is normal and acceptable is narrowly defined. And those furthest away from what is seen as normal are most likely to be targets of violence. Living passively with the status quo, maintaining what those with political and economic power deem acceptable, is a survival tactic for many. Others use the status quo actively, to seek to gain from oppression of others. My beliefs today have evolved because I made a conscious choice, often as a result of direct agitation, to see through different lenses. Just as importantly, I had access to knowledgeable people and to information that allowed me to think through different ideas and realities. A lens is a good metaphor since in its literal sense changing it changes the way its viewer sees the world. And the metaphorical lenses we choose are crucial, having the power to magnify, create better focus, and correct our vision.

In my first years as an activist and working as an organizer, my level of understanding came from viewing through someone else's lens. I had learned about how to understand structural racism as a college student at a predominantly white university. I had one Black feminist teacher in my first sixteen years of schooling. I first heard the word "capitalism," I recall, through readings on economics and history documentaries. I received formal community organizing training from experienced organizers who worked within the Alinsky tradition, working as an apprentice at Virginians Organized for Interfaith Community Engagement (VOICE), an Industrial Area Foundation (IAF) affiliate. To this day, I carry many of the organizing habits I learned from Martin Trimble and Kathleen O'Toole. Even then, I knew that my training was not enough. I knew something was missing.

As a result, I intentionally sought Black feminist sources in order to understand my experiences as a Black woman and connect them to the world's biggest and oldest systems of oppression. The Black feminist movement (and the fruit of its labor) taught me to understand the value of politics connected to lived experiences. As I developed a deeper understanding of myself and of the challenges facing Black organizing, I also gained understanding of the role of lesbian, bisexual, gay, transgender, and queer movements for liberation. Because of this I don't understand feminisms that support war, capitalism, transphobia, homophobia, anti-choice reproductive care, anti-Black racism, prisons, or police. In the process of working alongside brilliant young Black people to build BYP100, I made sense of my queerness. Together we made a choice to embody the best of the Black radical tradition while working hard to avoid mistakes and choices that didn't serve our desire to be free.

To this day, I don't remember the first time BYP100 used the phrase "organizing through a Black queer feminist lens." What I do remember is that the decision was made very early in our formation and not in a vacuum. We drew heavily on Black radical and feminist traditions. Our work follows a lineage of Black women, feminists, gay men, queer and transgender folks, disabled people, and formerly and currently incarcerated freedom fighters. None of us woke up knowing what we knew then or understand now. It's not common for most people in the United States to attend schools where the story of our freedom struggles and victories are as important as reading Ernest Hemingway, learning algebra, or understanding photosynthesis. We had to unlearn before we learned—and this continues today. We are in an ongoing process of defining the Black queer feminist lens and how it works.

As I define it, the Black queer feminist (BQF) lens is a political praxis (practice and theory) based in Black feminist and LGBTQ traditions and knowledge, through which people and groups see to bring their full selves into the process of dismantling all systems of oppression. By using this lens, we are aided in creating alternatives of self-governance and self-determination, and by using it we can more effectively prioritize problems and methods that center historically marginalized people in our communities. It is an aspiration and liberatory politic that Black folks must take up for the sake of our collective liberation and acts on the basic notion that none of us will be free unless all of us are free. Organizing through a BQF lens is inherently collaborative and not antagonistic to other radical feminisms or liberatory politics and practices. It specifically honors Black feminist and LGBTQ liberation movements. Taking up a Black queer feminist praxis of community organizing recognizes those who came before us and helps us see where we want to go.

For some of us who organize through a Black queer feminist lens, this is solely about politics and building power. For some, our work is derived from and rooted in personal identity as a queer person or as a Black feminist. But it requires us all to have politics that value identity and lived experiences. "Queer" isn't simply another word for being gay, lesbian, or bisexual. "Queer," as I am defining it here, represents a continuum of possibilities outside of what are considered to be normal sexual or gender identities and behaviors. Affirmation of queerness creates possibility outside the norm. My good friend and comrade Jessica Byrd once remarked that it was in queerness that she felt the world had endless possibilities. And in more ways than one, blackness is inherently queer.

I understand queer politics as laid out by Cathy Cohen in her article "Punks, Bulldaggers and Welfare Queens," which holds out the radical potential for liberation for all while honoring its origins to those deemed deviant for their race, gender, and sexuality.[7] Ultimately, using a Black queer feminist lens is a critical intervention, whether in conversations, organizing, and or in envisioning movement building toward Black liberation.

Those who use the BQF lens oppose queer activists who espouse liberal, individualistic, and white supremacist politics. Activists who have entered movement work in the second decade of the new millennium may have missed a few things as a result of hyper-reactionary tendencies after police killings and the plethora of injustices enacted upon Black people. Far too many people have come in thinking that activism is solely about what the individual wants to do, who the individual is, and what the individual believes should be done. Our movement would benefit if each person took a moment to reflect. The work is only as strong as the people with whom we work. Lone wolves in movement work can move fast, but can only advance transformative change as far as they are connected with people. Paris Hatcher, Black feminist leader, blames the neoliberal identity politics in today's movement on white queers' presence in movement spaces, self-absorbed people who promote individualism over collective struggle. Organizing by using the Black queer feminist lens calls for us to be individuals and to work collectively, with neither being at the expense of the other.

What we believe to be true matters for our movements. What we believe impacts how we move in the world, what we imagine is possible, what we choose to fight for, and what we fight against. But believing in something is never enough. We must turn our beliefs into collective action.

BYP100 Statement on Radical Inclusivity, 2014

BYP100 is a space where your Blackness is your own. We know that Blackness comprises several identities.

BYP100 is not only unapologetically Black, but also unapologetically queer, feminist/womanist, and sex positive. We do not blame any instance of sexual violence on victims/survivors.

BYP100 does not advocate "respectability politics," meaning we do not look to the middle class for examples for how Black people should dress or act.

BYP100 does not adopt or accept practices which assume that all Black people are heterosexual, cis-bodied, or able-bodied.

BYP100 strives to include Black people from various economic backgrounds and citizenship statuses.

BYP100 takes a radically inclusive approach to organizing by supporting/creating campaigns that focus on interlocking oppressions of marginalized peoples.

BYP100 believes that Black families do not have to look a certain way.

COMMUNITY ORGANIZING THROUGH A BLACK QUEER FEMINIST LENS

It is probably a truism that practicing any set of values is much more difficult than simply saying one believes in those values. This is especially true in movement spaces where lofty ideas reign and where structures for accountability do not always exist. While I have for years wrestled with figuring out what real accountability looks like, that challenge was actualized, with little room for hesitation, on

November 25, 2015, after I received a report that Malcolm London had sexually assaulted a young Black woman about three years earlier. At the time, in 2015, Malcolm was one of the BYP100 Chicago chapter co-chairs, a visible leader in the organization, and a popular poet.

What follows is my personal account about what happened, which I have never shared in writing and only discussed in a very limited way in public. The much longer story, from the perspectives of people more directly impacted, has been shared publicly.[8] I have to emphasize how excruciating it is for me to write about what happened following Malcolm's arrest. I'm choosing to do so because my hope is that our approach can be a case study for how our communities can develop more holistic and helpful responses to all forms of sexual violence.

The night before I received the report, on November 24, 2015, Malcolm was kidnapped and arrested by the Chicago Police Department (CPD) during the Justice for Laquan McDonald protests BYP100 Chicago had organized with Assata's Daughters, Fearless Leading by the Youth (FLY), the #LetUsBreathe Collective, and the Black Lives Matter Chicago chapter. After the kidnapping, Malcolm was wrongfully charged with felony battery against a police officer. We used social media and word of mouth to engage thousands of people. Across the country, people spread the story of his arrest, amplified the local call for his freedom, and contributed thousands of dollars to bail him out. Many of these people also followed media coverage of the police killing of seventeen-year-old Laquan McDonald and the subsequent CPD cover-up. Chicago and its organizing community entered center stage in national and international stories about policing in the United States.

The following day, while gathering the funds to bail him out and as the "Free Malcolm" campaign continued, I began to see tweets reporting that Malcolm had sexually assaulted someone. I also became aware of an open letter to BYP100 from the assault survivor posted on Facebook. I then contacted the person who sent some of the tweets and asked if I could be connected to the survivor.

It didn't take long for me and other BYP100 leaders to understand that our organization was about to be in the national spotlight, where its integrity would be questioned. The first person I spoke with was Rose Afriyie, BYP100's first national membership chair. From there, we spoke with other BYP100 leaders, including Fresco Steez, and began to form a plan of action. While wrapping our heads around the reports we also had to figure out the status of Malcolm's charges, deliver the news of the reports to him, and bail him out.

I remember that painful time vividly. I was so scared. The evening before, I had been shaking with anxiety because Malcolm was being held at Cook County Jail. I didn't know what was going to happen to him. Now, a day later, things had entirely changed. When I arrived at the courthouse, it was packed with folks demanding Malcolm's immediate release. I had never dealt with anything so intense and explosive, and I was holding back the information about the report of sexual assault.

I was in the hallway waiting to get in when we saw a comrade come out in tears. I thought the worst had happened to Malcolm, but instead all of his charges had been dropped. Relieved, I left the courthouse and walked over to Cathy Cohen, who was standing outside waiting for us to come out. I also remember talking then to Mariame Kaba, who would later support us in determining next steps. Distraught and in tears, I told them both about the tweets and asked their advice. And I realized that I was going to have to be the person to tell Malcolm news that would rock his world.

As I stood outside the courthouse, in tears, Malcolm walked out to cheers and screams. Supporters were all so elated, as if a Christmas miracle had transpired. After Malcolm addressed the media, Rose, Fresco, and I went over and walked him from the celebration. I'll never forget his face. I wondered if he'd ever been happier. For my part, I'd never been sadder, angrier, and more fearful, and my body and spirit felt the weight of what Rose, Fresco, and I had to do.

Rose, Fresco, and I were survivors of sexual violence from men—and we had decided to handle Malcolm with care. We needed to be compassionate, but I felt pain, as if I'd been hit in the gut. It was hard to not just say, "Fuck this dude; he ain't worth it." But we didn't walk away.

I trust Black women—always. The internal conflict and dialogue looping through my mind told me that we needed to disown our brother, and it also told me that we had to hold our sister, a Black woman accusing Malcolm of assault, with compassion, even though we didn't know her. Our politics told us that a survivor-led process was required; our experiences as women told us that it was neces-sary. We delivered the news to Malcolm as he sat in the back of my compact car. Malcolm was shocked and deflated as he recounted his memory of what had happened.

The next weekend Rose and I met with Kyra, the survivor. Flanked by two friends, Kyra recounted what had happened with Malcolm. We listened, and I left feeling somewhat numb and very unsure about what actually had happened and how to move forward. Questioning how her story varied from his and working to maintain our commitment to a survivor-led process, I doubted my own values as a Black feminist.

We did not have a full tool kit to deal with such a complicated and difficult situation. One of our organization's leaders, a popular, straight Black man, had been scooped up by the Chicago Police Department, putting our organization center stage at the same time that a Black woman was accusing him of sexual assault. Chicago's mayor, police superintendent, and the police in general were then under a national spotlight. Despite a lack of experience in negotiating this terrain, our community had expertise and people willing to help move us through a survivor-led process of transformative justice. Malcolm was placed on a membership hiatus, and BYP100 leaders began to develop plans for internal structural changes to address and prevent harm within our organization. Malcolm and Kyra committed to a transformative justice process led by experienced practitioners, something that required over a year of work, with deep community support. I am grateful for Kyra, Malcolm, Mariame Kaba, Mayadet Cruz, Xavier Danae MaatRa, and the community members who led the process.

While BYP100 had not even existed when the assault took place, our organization and its leaders chose to be accountable to the survivor and the broader community. In the days following Malcolm's arrest and in the transformative justice process, I came to realize what it meant to embody Black queer feminism as a praxis. The way was not easy but full of twists, turns, and missteps, resulting in changes in the people involved and structural changes within our organization.

The experience with Malcolm was not the last crisis we would face as an organization. We received a wide range of public critique and support. People questioned whether our organization and its leaders (mostly Black women) could handle a survivor-led process. We were criticized by people who had not spoken with Rose or me or anyone else at BYP100. A chorus of activists inside and outside of the organization held us responsible for the actions of a Black man that took place before the organization even existed. It was because of our stated values that people called us to task. We took a great risk in a moment when our organization had never been more visible. I, as a leader, had never been more visible, and Chicago was in the spotlight after the release of the video depicting Laquan McDonald's execution by police. I feel strongly that few people understood the potential firestorm of that moment, when we were held to standards that I had never witnessed before.

We made it through that time—and we continue today—because of the deep love of BYP100 leaders and elders who responded with

patience and wisdom. And for me there are lessons for our movement in those events. First, you must understand that trusting Black
women is not common practice. Black women are consistently den-
igrated, treated as and seen as liars, whores, and strong enough for
anything. Black women are told, encouraged, and sometimes forced
to play very limited roles in society and in social justice movements.

As a movement, we cannot jump to defend anyone accused of
sexual violence without compassion for the person (or people) reporting having been harmed. The worst of the culture created by
gender-based oppression shows up when sexual violence occurs.
Almost no one will believe survivors at first, and some will never
believe them. I've witnessed Black women support people who are
accused of sexual violence, taking their side without any evident solidarity or compassion or support for Black women accusers, and it has
broken my heart.

No one should be discarded or disowned, and we had to decide
to stick with both Kyra and Malcolm, despite calls by many that we
wash our hands of them both. The truth is also that women, more often than not, have to deal with the fallout after such crises. In our organization, women have primarily had to manage the crisis of sexual
violence accusations, thus they have been most criticized publicly,
especially on Facebook, for what does and does not happen in their
aftermath. When it comes to sexual violence accusations in queer
relationships, particularly with two people of the same gender, this
becomes even more complex. Oftentimes, power dynamics are not as
clear, and neither is the articulation of harm. Women seen as being
masculine can be abused by women seen as feminine. There is no
rulebook once we introduce queer relationships into the discussion.

So many women in our movement have experienced sexual
trauma and have never received restoration from a perpetrator. Survivors are asked to accept and do the most impossible, unreasonable,
and painful things every day. So I understand the impulse to react

with extreme doubt and frustration. What I ask is that we habitually practice compassion for everyone in our movement. All too often our responses to our people mirror our responses to the state. Our comrades should not become our targets.

The Black queer feminist lens at its best shows us the full humanity of those in our community, even when our own humanity is not fully recognized in the broader world. But our work requires systems and institutions, and none of it is easy or comfortable. In 2016, BYP100 formed its National Healing and Safety Council to generate transformative accountability processes in cases where there has been hurt and harm involving a BYP100 member. This self-governing body does our prevention and intervention work. The Healing and Safety Council holds potential and promise for our organization, and if we get it right it will benefit the entire movement. Like the development of a child, there have been many bumps and falls and mistakes along the way.

Black queer feminism as a praxis is full of contradictions because we are people working to practice and explain what it means. I have muddied the water on this topic, and BYP100 has too. Each of us falls short of living the politics we commit to, and there is always more work to do so that the trauma and violence we experience through systemic oppression no longer exists. Did we set ourselves up for failure by opening a space that espouses values no one can completely live up to? I can accept that.

We are fighting for our lives against formidable enemies, but we are optimistic and steadfast in the idea that we can learn to treat each other better. We are participating in various projects of abolition—abolition of prison, abolition of capitalism, and abolition of patriarchal violence. We are practicing and theorizing as we go. We are seeking to eradicate oppressive systems in the world. And all our effort is worth it.

CHAPTER 2

REVIVING THE BLACK RADICAL IMAGINATION

*What are today's young activists dreaming about? We know what
they are fighting against, but what are they fighting for?*

—ROBIN D. G. KELLEY, *Freedom Dreams*

Contemporary Black youth-led rebellions and organizations are evidence that Robin Kelley's questions in his 2002 book *Freedom Dreams*
are still germane. It is an ongoing project: "What are today's young
activists dreaming about? We know what they are fighting against,
but what are they fighting for?" Whether or not we possess ancestral
memory and knowledge of our predecessors, young Black activists
in the United States and abroad embody the new wave of the Black
radical tradition. The Black radical tradition comprises cultural and
intellectual work aimed at disrupting oppressive political, economic,
and social norms, and its roots are in anticolonial and antislavery efforts of centuries past. Our work builds on the legacies of the Haitian
Revolution, Maroon societies in the Caribbean, *quilombos* of Brazil,
the Student Nonviolent Coordinating Committee (SNCC), and the
Combahee River Collective. We are dreaming about and fighting for
a world without prisons, without gender-based violence, where definitions of valuable work are transformed, and where the land we live

on is liberated alongside its peoples. The formations through which we work to build this movement are diverse, and we include people within and outside of organizations, scholars and intellectuals within and outside of the academy, and community organizers. We are a movement of many leaders with a structural analysis of oppression advancing a multi-issue struggle to transform the world.

Some say that today's Black liberation movement has no vision or plan, no meaningful experiences, as a basis. They are skeptical of today's crop of activists and our pluralistic approach to movement building and see our activism as short-lived. Others see a movement that is both a part of a long historical tradition and the beginning of a new era. Based on my study of history and involvement in Black liberation work for more than twelve years, I am siding with the latter.

This contemporary era of the Black liberation struggle approaches the dismantling of capitalism, patriarchy, and anti-Blackness in new ways while still being grounded in earlier movements. Our work revisits the boundaries of gender and blackness and challenges binaries of male or female, lesbian/gay/bisexual/queer or straight, and transgender or cisgender. None of these binaries hold true when it comes to Black people, yet we must still confront and reconcile identities rife with contradictions. This new approach, employed over a sustained period, is grounds to validate this as a movement and not simply a moment in time.

The precise beginning of this era is debatable. Was it on September 20, 2007, when over fifteen thousand people rallied in a small Louisiana town in support of the "Jena 6," after six Black teenage boys were charged with attempted murder after beating a white schoolmate? Did it start in the summer of 2011 at the height of a decades-long fight to save Troy Davis from a state-sanctioned death sentence after his unjust conviction for murdering a police officer? Or was it the national mobilizations sparked by the killing of Trayvon Martin by a neighborhood vigilante in Florida in February 2012 and the killer's subsequent acquittal on grounds of self-defense? Some may argue it was the historical uprising sparked by the militarized response in the small town Ferguson, Missouri, after the August 9, 2014, killing of Mike Brown by a Ferguson police officer. Was it the aftermath of Hurricane Katrina or one of the other countless police shootings that motivated mass public action?

We may not agree on when this movement era began, but we must come to terms with the context in which it exists. This movement is active in a period when Black people are living under the heels of a neoliberal state, a global crisis of capitalism, and further entrenchment of anti-Blackness through policy and culture alike. It is a time of unprecedented levels of state surveillance, unequal and questionable definitions of terrorism, and an obscene expansion of the military-industrial complex. The circumstances we face today are largely the result of decades of decisions to solidify the control of the government by a ruling class of wealthy elites. The consequences of those decisions affect ordinary people, the economy, the earth's ecology, and, yes, our movement too.

Amid global crises including clean water shortages, an ongoing war in Afghanistan, forced migrations, and mass housing instability, this generation of activists operates within a historical era. We are the first era of the larger Black freedom movement to experience a political terrain that included a Black US president. The election of Barack Obama raised so much hope and signaled change to our people and to the world. I'd be a liar if I did not admit to feeling moments of joy as the Obamas took up residence in Washington, DC.

Unprecedented legislation, albeit far from perfect, passed during Obama's tenure as president. The Affordable Care Act (better known as "Obamacare") opened access to health care for twenty million uninsured people. Obama's administration began working to normalize relations with Cuba. He granted clemency to political prisoners, including Chelsea Manning and Oscar Lopez. The Obama administration was full of brilliant and talented people—including many Black and LGBTQ folks who provided valuable leadership, a fact I will not discount or undersell in my read of where we are today. But I'm clear that our way forward cannot stay in a place of comfortable reminiscing. We have to go deeper.

If we are willing to hold on to the symbolism of Obama's presidency and its progress, then we must also contend with its violence and regression. Barack Obama was a war president and led an administration that deported more undocumented immigrants than any previous one. The civil rights establishment failed to criticize Obama for this, which I find appalling. I watched as individuals and organizations, lauded as the voice of Black America, failed to advance a clear agenda to improve the lives of our people and provide a clear pipeline to leadership roles for the growing masses of young Black activists mobilized in the aftermath of police killings. I share the angst of many who saw themselves outside of the established organizations such as the NAACP, the National Urban League, and the National Action Network. As the Obama years passed, the critiques of his administration grew, even if unevenly and inadequately.

I heard repeatedly, "Obama was elected to represent all Americans, not just Black people." I heard almost as often, "If he can pass legislation for LGBT people and immigrants, then he can do something for Black people." Black women showed up as Obama campaign staff, as volunteers, and on Election Day with the highest turnout rate of any Democratic voter constituency. Obama gained over 90 percent of the Black vote in his 2008 and 2012 elections. Now that Obama is out of office, we in the "all Americans" bloc still have every right to expect accountability from any U.S. president. Republicans did not cease to advance their party goals after a Democrat won the presidency. Why should we do differently?

There are Black LGBT people and Black immigrants (and those who are both) fighting for all of those issues. Black freedom dreams and freedom fighting have always entailed multiple issues. Black people have consistently taken action as LGBTQ people, as immigrants, as women, as disabled people, as refugees, and as poor people. Virtually all the problems of the world affect Black people throughout the African diaspora. Elected officials hold too much power over our lives, and we must think bigger and hold their feet to the fire.

The Obama administration did not lead the advancement of radical Black politics in the twenty-first century. He was the leader of a nation-state that remains deeply entrenched in politics of imperialism and self-interested intervention, a nation-state with a population of white people increasingly afraid of losing their hold on power. His administration's record shows both meaningful reforms and entrenchment of capitalist policy, confirming that Black politics and politicians are not inherently radical or transformative. Transformative change, meaning change that dismantles oppressive systems and fundamentally shifts power into the hands of communities, takes time. That is what this new era of movement has had to contend with—the contradiction of progress and transformation. Transformation is what we need, but reform is what was offered time and time again by the Obama administration.

Our young movement is constantly confronting this contradiction along with many others. We were met with questions of how to fund the work. Should our organizations become nonprofits for the sake of fund-raising, or should we develop other structures? What do we do with hyper-visible activists with politics that actively thwart radical agendas? Also, as I wrote in chapter 1, we struggle with issues of accountability in the aftermath of sexual violence. This dynamic, while situated in a unique context, is normal for any liberation movement.

Movements ebb and advance. There are flash points, everyday people with visions, and mass actions that happen with and without planning. Yes, movements have architecture. They also require spontaneity and their participants experience moments of deep uncertainty and contradiction. The pursuit of freedom and collective liberation is never linear because humanity is too complex for that. Human history and progress do not make up a neat chain of events. A movement can be catalyzed through moments of deep tragedy as well as through victories. Young activists and organizers, like our movement elders, live within the tension between the world as it is and the world as it we think should be. Likewise our work may or may not fit expectations of how movement building should happen. I remember a SNCC veterans meeting I attended in 2015. The disconnect between generations there was wide. There was a moment when we had to demonstrate that our organizing used many of the same tactics our elders had deployed during the civil rights movement. At the time, some did not realize that door-knocking and canvassing were tactics of the present and not just the past.

Our history of resistance shows what oppressed humans will do when freedom and collective liberation are on the horizon. Our resistance is richly textured, and our tactics range from armed rebellion and self-defense to various forms of noncooperation (e.g., sit-ins and boycotts) to cultural preservation—all under various threats of violence. Knowing we are part of the Black radical tradition, young Black people feel a duty to fight for our freedom, as directed by Assata Shakur. This responsibility is both a birthright and a burden.

At its best, the Black radical tradition represents the deepest of our thinking and the most effective action for Black liberation. This tradition includes those who saw the system around them and believed that it could be dismantled and completely transformed. Black feminism, communism, socialism, liberation theology, and hip-hop are all part of the Black radical tradition and have transformed the shape of Black struggle and life by influencing thought and action. At its worst, this tradition addresses race while failing to advance the destruction of all class and gender hierarchies. It has produced mass organizing where women have been quarantined to do the work deemed beneath men. It has ousted people who are LGBTQ, not college-educated, or otherwise considered not respectable. Radical movements can do awful things in the name of liberation, often under the premise that the ends justify the means.

Black folks living under slavery and colonialism and in its aftermath have always imagined that freedom and liberation were possible. Here the distinction between freedom and liberation is that of individual freedom versus collective access to our full humanity. The former can be gained and felt on various levels, but the latter is an ongoing process. We can gain or hold various freedoms—for example, the freedom to vote, the freedom to marry, the freedom to choose abortion. But liberation is a collective effort in which, even after freedoms are won, continual regeneration and transformation are necessary. Liberation must entail resistance to the dominant oppressive systems that permeate our societies (e.g., capitalism, patriarchy, and anti-Black racism).

Thus there is constant tension, constant struggle. There are always forces, sometimes even within a social justice movement, that fight to kill the imagination of those actively engaged in the struggle (and for that matter to limit all thinking about radical possibilities). But oppressed people have always imagined that freedom is possible, and their imagination will not be vanquished. The Black radical tradition requires an ongoing and persistent cultivation of the Black radical imagination. It is within the spaces of imagination, the dream spaces, that liberatory practices are born and grow, leading to the space to act and to transform.

KILLING THE BLACK IMAGINATION

Like many people in social justice movements, I learned about generic racism and white privilege in school and in organizations before

I learned about anti-Blackness and anti-Black racism. I also learned about racism before I learned about patriarchy and capitalism. While white supremacy, patriarchy, and capitalism affect everyone, Black people are uniquely oppressed. Anti-Blackness is a system of beliefs and practices that attack, erode, and limit the humanity of Black people. It was cultivated through the transatlantic slave trade and continues today in the policies and practices of nation-states, corporations, individuals, and entire societies. Anti-Blackness, broadly, is the belief that there is something wrong with Black people, that we are not full human beings. That might sound extreme, but history and the present hold countless examples of the dehumanization of Black people—in print, films, advertising, and virtually all forms of expression.

Anti-Blackness works 24/7 to kill the Black imagination. This takes place when our children are required to attend schools with no art and music programs. It takes place when Black women's hairstyles are deemed unprofessional, "ghetto," or simply ugly. The destructiveness is ongoing, chronic, but it is manifested acutely. It tells our children to dream of a better future instead of a better *now*, in the communities where they live. The killing of the Black imagination happens when we are told we should aspire to work downtown and not on the corner next to where we live. Killing the Black imagination is both place-based and psychological. It permeates what we watch on television and read on social media.

Black folks have always been vulnerable to violence by state-supported individuals and institutions. And what it means to be Black in the world manifests differently depending on one's location and other factors. In a lecture by Frank Wilderson in 2011, the scholar and activist laid out arguments (citing Orlando Patterson, Saidiya Hartman, and Hortense Spillers) that Black people are perpetual slaves-in-waiting. This status entails the imminent threat of physical, psychic, or spiritual violence and the lack of control over one's body. It entails bearing the brunt of actions that diminish one's ability to live fully and even to be perceived as fully human. For Black folks in the US, the threat of violence persists regardless of what we do or do not do.

Saidiya Hartman's work highlights how the violence Black people experience doesn't require consent or reason. When someone rebels, an opposing force will strike back. There's a reaction to every action. But with Anti-Blackness you will get hit even if you don't rebel. Black people are repeatedly told that there's something inherently criminal about us and that we deserve to be hit. There's something about us. "Well, you didn't work hard enough," we hear, and sometimes those words are spoken by a Black person. "You don't speak English well enough." You didn't go to the right schools. You don't have the proper education. You should be straight! "Why are you so gay?" "Why are you so trans?" "Why are you so queer?" We live in a country where people work forty or more hours a week and still live in poverty because they don't earn a living wage, so it's never simply about working hard enough. Meritocracy is a lie.

Anti-Blackness is inextricably tied to the mass criminalization of Black people. Criminalization is a process where a person is incriminated for actions that wouldn't be deemed criminal if done by a white, wealthy, or otherwise privileged person. The person who killed seventeen-year-old Trayvon Martin assumed that Trayvon was not supposed to be in the neighborhood. He assumed that a tall Black boy wearing a hoodie was not supposed to be there and was up to no good. He took it upon himself to act, and he ultimately took Trayvon's life. That is anti-Blackness. That is anti-Black racism specifically. Trayvon was not a white boy in a hoodie. He was not a white-passing Latino in a hoodie. He was not an Asian in a hoodie. Trayvon was a Black boy in a hoodie. And so Trayvon was killed.

I've seen things in my life that I will never forget. As a result, I've learned that humans have a tremendous capacity for acting violently.

Packed away in my memories are images of apartheid, institutionalized control, and collective punishment. I packed them deeply, but they come up at the most unwanted times. Walking past National Guard troops standing in front of City Hall during the Baltimore uprising of 2015 took me back to a confrontation comrades and I experienced while traveling to the occupied territories of Palestine. The presence of a force that you know has the power to assault and even kill you with impunity induces fear, intimidation, and terror. I don't ever want to get used to seeing armed soldiers walking among ordinary people trying to live their lives. Yet this is reality for oppressed people around the world.

COLLECTIVE PUNISHMENT

I traveled to Ghana in 2016 with my comrade Janae Bonsu, and my world was rocked. Standing in Elmina Castle's slave dungeons, I felt a disconnect as I witnessed people make jokes and laugh throughout the tour. Through it all, I felt that I was missing something while in Ghana. Yes, I was learning about human resistance and culture-making, but I was far from home, far from the Great Migration, the creation of jazz, and the culinary traditions my ancestors carried. I realized that I had at best a superficial understanding of how Blackness in the US is connected to Blackness elsewhere in the Americas and in the world. I became hungry to learn. Beatriz Beckford, a friend and comrade, told me that my experience in Ghana was similar to Saidiya Hartman's story as told in her book *Lose Your Mother: A Journey Along the Atlantic Slave Route*. The contradictions of seeking where I come from in Africa while not knowing enough about Black life history in the US South agitated me into a new commitment. Descendants of enslaved Africans are too often taught to be ashamed of our past. We are encouraged to skip over what has happened. The dungeons of Elmina Castle in Ghana jolted me, in fact traumatized me, and I needed to ask new questions about my identity and where I come from. There are lessons to be learned from a people who survived and created under centuries of unconsciona-ble violence.

I am the daughter of the enslaved Africans forcibly brought to the Western Hemisphere. There is no me without the journey of my ancestors across the Atlantic. The same can be said of all my people today. The same can be said of my mother, my grandmother, and *her* mother. Our ancestors fought and managed to hold on to Indigenous traditions while also creating new ones. They embodied resilience. Freedom-dreaming is one of the most significant things any human can do. The Black radical tradition begins with the dreams of our ancestors, who were the first to fight against colonialism and what became the transatlantic slave trade.

The struggle for Black liberation has always been global. Full of contradictions, enslaved Africans forged movements that were hyper-local but that also transcended enforced borders. In part, they were responding (as we continue today to respond) to the collec-tive punishment of Black people. I first learned about the idea of collective punishment in the Palestinian context while traveling through the occupied territories of Palestine with a delegation orga-nized by Dr. Maytha Alhassen and Dream Defenders cofounder Ah-mad Abuznaid. Throughout several conversations with people living there, collective punishment was described to me as the violence, control, and apartheid Palestinians were subjected to, on that land and throughout the Palestinian diaspora, under the Israeli regime, regardless of their individual actions.

Collective punishment has also been used to describe war crimes against political prisoners and entire ethnic groups. In this context, collective punishment is seen as violent acts committed against a person or a group due to the actions of others. Article 33 of the United Nations Geneva Convention of 1949 says that, in the time of war,

> No protected person may be punished for an offence he or she has not personally committed. Collective penalties and likewise all measures of intimidation or of terrorism are prohibited.
>
> Pillage is prohibited.
>
> Reprisals against protected persons and their property are prohibited.

War has evolved since this document was adopted. Twentieth-century war involved combatants and technology different from those of today, but they entailed colonialism and capitalism just as now. Today the United States engages in wars of ideas, which play out in real time—and real bloodshed—in individuals around the world. Just who is on the offense and who is on the defense is not always as neat as who shot first. For example, the "War on Drugs," the "War on Crime," and the "War on Terror" each play out across geographies and along lines of race, class, and gender. Today, wars have evolved from the trope of the "superpredator" Black and Brown child theorized by Princeton scholar John Dilulio and popularized by such people as Hillary and Bill Clinton, and the Black "welfare queen" said to be defrauding state budgets, to the criminalization of Muslims and Arabs and bombing of Arab nations.

Black freedom fighters have been consistently targeted and killed and imprisoned by the US government under claims of national security threat. Some have escaped to live in exile. As an extension of the wars on terrorism and crime, young Black people like Ferguson freedom fighter Josh Williams, who was sentenced to eight years in prison, are used as examples to deter direct action. Assata Shakur's unjust imprisonment and torture in 1977 illustrates state repression of Black activists that is not just racialized but gendered. Shakur, who was liberated in 1979 and made her way to Cuba, is called a terrorist and remains on the FBI Most Wanted list, with a million-dollar bounty for her capture.

The FBI counterterrorism division's "Black Identity Extremist" (BIE) designation, reported in October 2017, adds today's Black activists to the government's list of national security threats. According to a report in *Foreign Policy*, "The FBI assesses it is very likely Black Identity Extremist (BIE) perceptions of police brutality against African Americans spurred an increase in premeditated, retaliatory lethal violence against law enforcement."[1] Despite weak evidence connecting violent acts to Black activists, and despite former FBI counterterrorism officials expressing shock over the designation and saying that it has no basis, the FBI has defended its position. While it may be tempting to brush off the "BIE" label as a distraction, our movement should take this seriously. As Black women and LGBTQ folks continue to be on the front lines and highly visible, we should consider how the BIE designation increases vulnerability and the likelihood of racialized and gendered oppression.

As the government expands its war tactics, our definitions of collective punishment must broaden too. The ongoing oppression of Afro-Palestinians and people of African descent in the occupied territories is enabled by the same systems of punishment, mass criminalization, and surveillance that oppress Black people globally. The Israeli occupation perpetuates the global practice of anti-Blackness, and anti-Blackness perpetuates the collective punishment of Afro-Palestinians and other people of African descent on that land. I chewed on this concept for some time before I began to speak about it publicly. It is important to take great care and not compare oppression. That does not serve the goal of collective liberation. No one, besides our oppressors, wins in an argument about who got whipped the worst. Eradicating oppression requires us to identify connections, not sameness.

The broadening of international applications of collective punishment to include anti-Blackness is an invitation to make deeper connections. Historian Liam Hogan and a team of researchers created a mapping project to track white mob violence, riots, and pogroms against Black communities. They identified this violence as collective punishment and emphasized violence by white people against Black people in the US that was "meant to terrorize the wider community."[2] Rumors, claims of disrespect, and labor competition—all of these have led to violence. This is how anti-Blackness plays out—it doesn't require reason.

We can and must go deeper with definitions of collective punishment. Just as it is imperative to understand the struggle for Palestinian liberation as a Black queer and feminist issue, we must understand and recognize how anti-Blackness shows up in the collective punishment of Palestinians. The forced sterilization of East African women should be a central topic in global and local conversations about what it will take to end the Israeli occupation. Palestine will not be free until all the oppressed people living under the apartheid regime are free. In this case, the group of actors complicit in the ongoing oppression is varied and includes government officials and private individuals (in some instances, Palestinians who advance interests of the Israeli state). Developing a more complete story of what's happening to oppressed people globally expands our ability to craft better strategies for creating transformative change.

THE FISTS OF CAPITALISM AND PATRIARCHY: ANTI-BLACKNESS AND GENDERED VIOLENCE

Governments and corporations are not the only arbiters of violence against Black people. We experience and commit violence against each other within our homes, communities, and the institutions we interact with daily. It goes beyond the mainstream myth of so-called Black-on-Black crime. That story ignores the forces that create conditions of poverty and fragile mental and physical health. It ignores the individuals who profit from gun violence. It says little about how toxic masculinity informs our ideas about manhood, womanhood, and respect. It ignores the impact of the drug crisis throughout Black communities in the US The story of Black-on-Black crime points the finger at individuals and fails to give more than lip service to the root causes of violence. The violence within Black communities can be eradicated by Black people but only if done in tandem with dismantling the systems of capitalism and patriarchy. Our people will continue to die in cages, in homes, in hospitals, and on the streets if we fail to accept that both are killing us.

Violence is a constant, systemic killer of possibility. Violence occurs on structural and interpersonal levels through abuse and harm that violates and diminishes people's ability to live with full dignity. Poverty is violence. Lack of autonomy over reproductive decisions is violence. Stripping away access to cultural practices and traditions that allow us to live with our human dignity is violence. Allowing rape to happen generation after generation is violence. The Black imagination is systemically killed through gender-based violence, criminalization and incarceration, poverty, and environmental degradation.

Anti-Blackness and gendered violence go hand in hand. They are not separate. Anti-violence activist and scholar Beth E. Richie makes it plain in the "violence matrix" she developed to explain the violence Black women experience and the responses needed to end it (see the table "Violence Matrix").

Richie writes, "Surrounding the violence matrix is the tangled web of structural disadvantages, institutionalized racism, gender domination, class exploitation, heteropatriarchy, and other forms of oppression that lock the abuse of Black women in place. Responses

VIOLENCE MATRIX

	Physical Assault	Sexual Assault	Social Disenfranchisement
Intimate Household	Direct physical assaults by intimate partners or household members; victim retaliation	Sexual aggression by intimate partners or household members	Emotional abuse and manipulation by intimate partners or household members, forced use of drug and alcohol, isolation, and economic abuse
Community	Assaults by neighbors, lack of bystander intervention, availability of weapons	Sexual harassment, acquaintance rape, gang rape, sex trafficking, stalking	Degrading comments, hostile neighborhood conditions, hostile or unresponsive school and work environments, residential segregation, lack of social capital, threat of violence
Social Sphere	Stranger assault, state violence (e.g., police), gun control policies	Stranger rape, coerced sterilization, unwanted exposure to pornography	Negative media images, denial of significance of victimization, degrading encounters with public agencies, victim blaming, lack of affordable housing, lack of employment and health care, mistrust of public agencies, poverty

need to be developed that take all of the forms of abuse and all of the spheres within which injustice occurs into account."[3]

Applying a Black queer feminist lens to our understanding of violence allows people concerned with collective liberation to have a deeper understanding of what is happening to our people. The lens helps us understand how state and interpersonal violence operate across our lives. The BQF lens enables us to see how violence within our homes, communities, and broader society are connected to the violence inflicted on us by the government and corporations. A more complete view of what happens in our lives will lead to real solutions instead of just bandages and work-arounds.

It is impossible to end the violence that Black people face from their intimate partners, family members, acquaintances, and strangers if we think we only need to combat police violence. On June 24, 2016, Jessica Hampton was stabbed to death by an ex-boyfriend while riding public transportation in Chicago. Family members witnessed the killing of Rae'Lynn Thomas by her mother's ex-boyfriend in Columbus, Ohio, in August 2016. These two women, one transgender, reflect what happens to Black women around the world every day.

The country I live in condones this by normalizing violence. It says that some people are not allowed self-determination, such as Black trans women trying to access health care or being required to have a government ID listing "correct" gender. Anti-Blackness perpetuates restrictive gender categories and norms that none of us can fully embody. The United States affirms, through law and budget allocations of hundreds of millions of dollars, that certain acts of violence against women are punishable by imprisonment and even death. But there are no such vast budget allocations for transformative transformative programs, mental health services, and intervention services that put power into the hands of communities instead of state-controlled institutions.

FREEDOM DREAMING

Blackness (and a people's proximity to it) is the fulcrum of racial and economic oppression in the Americas.[4] So much depends upon African slavery: ideas about property, marriage, and gender, to name just three. The transatlantic slave trade drove economic growth for colonial powers. There would be no US or European superpowers without the transport, enslavement, and exploited labor (agricultural and reproductive) of Africans. The slave trade meant profits and power not only for plantation owners but also for entire nations: Great Britain, France, Spain, and the United States. Thus laws were put into place to perpetuate it, laws virtually criminalizing the humanity of enslaved African people, criminalizing their very expressions of joy and tendency toward freedom. This is especially clear in the history of the militarized former colony of San Domingo—Haiti, as we know it today—the first independent Black nation in the Western Hemisphere. The story of Haiti's ongoing struggle for self-determination is essential to the story of the Black radical imagination and tradition, and it is a tale of uncomfortable truths, contradictions, and promise.

I imagine that those who took up arms to spark the 1804 Haitian Revolution cycled through various manifestations of what liberation could look like. I situate Haiti as a central example of the possibilities and contradictions of the Black radical imagination using Ella Baker's framework for radicalism: "In order for us as poor and oppressed people to become part of a society that is meaningful, the system under which we now exist has to be radically changed. This means that we are going to have to learn to think in radical terms. I use the term radical in its original meaning—getting down to and understanding the root cause. It means facing a system that does not lend itself to your needs and devising means by which you change that system."[5]

Haitian freedom fighters chose to strike directly at slavery, a system of domination amassing wealth for the French Crown and individual slave owners but not the many who did not own land or slaves.

The everyday people and militia who led the armed revolution envisioned a free Black nation in a region—the Caribbean—that otherwise comprised occupied territories reliant on slavery and marked by Native genocide. They also envisioned *living*. Before the revolution, Africans shipped to Haiti died within ten years on average.

The brutal system led to profits for colonizers and death for Black people. Enslaved Africans were worked to death, but at least a million lived long enough to rebel, overthrow the colonial authorities, and create the first Black republic in the Western Hemisphere. Enslaved and free Africans alike in Haiti had been inspired by what they had learned of the French Revolution. Having ousted the French, Black generals including Toussaint L'Ouverture and Jacques Dessalines then faced the task of nation-building. As news of the revolutionaries' success spread north, US slaveholders feared repercussions.

Might a seventh-generation enslaved African in pre-revolution Haiti have imagined living in a world without constant violence? A world where one's children belonged to one's own family and not to a slave master? What capacity of mind it would have meant to imagine this? Enslaved Africans had led revolts elsewhere in the Caribbean prior to the 1804 insurrection, but no other site of slavery was as notorious as Haiti for brutality and the disposability of the enslaved. No other French colony was as profitable as Haiti. And, most importantly, no other revolt resulted in the successful abolition of slavery.

Haiti is an example of what happens when Black people decide to be property no more. The Haitian Revolution disrupted the economic structure of three continents. Western superpowers including France, Great Britain, and the United States did not want a free Black nation surrounded by slave colonies, and they did almost everything they could to ensure that Haiti would be shackled by disease, poverty, and dependence, and it has been riddled with trauma and disasters ever since, many made worse by intentional decisions stunting its development. The story of Haiti illustrates that freedom movements guarantee struggle. Haiti's 1804 revolution embodies the potential of the Black imagination, but its aftermath is an example of systemic efforts to kill the Black imagination. The moment the revolution was successful, the forces of anti-Blackness began to punish Haiti.

Knowledge of Haitian history might have tempered expectations for the wave of Black mayors elected in the United States during the 1970s and 1980s. Perhaps a closer study of Haiti might have served as a fulcrum for nation-building in South Africa after its first democratic elections, where many expected an end to apartheid that has yet to come. Political representation without clear politics of collective liberation will lead to repeated cycles of failure.

THE REVIVAL IS NOW

The legendary actor Cicely Tyson used the analogy of a ladder to explain the social order of the world. On the ladder are white men, white women, Black men, and Black women. Black women are on the last rung, below everyone else. And we "still hold on, and that is our strength."[6] Yes, our strength can be found in struggle, but we have to aspire to more than struggle. And we have to find pride in the ability to create an entirely new ladder. Period. The killing of the Black imagination tells us that this one ladder is the only one we have. And the social order will not change as long as we believe that it is okay to just keep holding on to the bottom rung. As Tyson rightly noted, we're not only on the bottom rung but everyone above us keeps us down. And by "us" I'm referring to all Black women across marginalized statuses. Black women who are poor, refugees, incarcerated, transgender, undocumented immigrants, queer, or disabled may be barely holding on to the ladder.

We live in a world that tells Black women that we are incapable mothers, that we are insufficient athletes, and that we are incapable of rigorous intellectual production. And this is an attack on our ability to self-determine. Self-determination and the ability to move around this world should be rights for all. Where I diverge with Cicely Tyson is on whether holding on is our strength. The killing of the Black imagination, I believe, tells us that we must rise only as far as the world will allow us. This is my position, and this is what I'm gonna do. But I argue that Black women have always demanded and done more. I imagine that Ms. Tyson would say the same. We've never accepted that the bottom rung is where we will remain. And that's where the Black imagination lives. It lives in our ability to create alternatives, whether those are alternative economies, alternative family structures, or something else entirely.

We live in a time when young Black people in the United States have once again shifted the center of gravity in politics, kitchen table conversations, and mainstream media discourse. From Ferguson to Chicago, Charlotte, and Baltimore, uprisings of young Blacks have put the world on notice that something is shifting in the United States.

Young Black activists are no longer limiting themselves to party politics. We are using a hybrid of direct action tactics, traditional field organizing, and spiritual practices. Our actions are forcing liberals, progressives, and even radicals to reassess their roles in social justice work. We are called "radical," with the connotation of irrationality, something to be feared, because we demand a world without police and prisons. We are called reactionary because we refuse to be silent about the blood spilled on the streets by state-sanctioned violence. We are called exclusionary because we are unapologetically Black and queer and feminist. We are deemed unskilled and undisciplined because our organizing doesn't fit traditional modes. We are carrying on the legacy of Black vanguards such as freedom fighter Fannie Lou Hamer and Ballroom queen Crystal LaBeija by demanding more while virtually every major institution of power tells us that we are not fully human. Like those before us, we are met with violence.

It is important that we tell our own story and that it belongs to us and not to social media giants such as Twitter or Facebook. Too often the ideas behind social movements are popularized through media that activists do not control. Our work is historicized and analyzed by people who have not sat in jail cells with us, participated in countless organizing meetings, or developed and won campaigns with us. Far too many who pontificate about our work will never have to apply Black queer feminist theory to the actual practice of movement building.

Now is the time for young Black community organizers on the ground to challenge the mostly white, mostly male, and mostly cisgender and heterosexual narratives on the whys and hows of building a social movement. In this post-Obama era, it is crucial that we read about how to organize and how to build a movement from those who are actually doing it. Many people are thinking and writing about the past and predicting what will come next. One thing is clear: the movement work happening right now will play a major role in what shape this society takes next. We have the responsibility and ability as organizers and activists to deepen our collective political education work, to take the lead in generating public thought and discussion—and we can do so with our own words. We don't have to wait on academics and journalists to investigate our work and dictate our next steps. We have the power to do that ourselves. Future generations shouldn't have to look to historians and political scientists to explain our thinking. We need to make it clear ourselves.

We exist in a lineage of Maroons, rebels, and revolutionaries, people who decided to live free or die, as the motto goes, since the first enslaved Africans were brought to the Americas. While our struggle is not new, the dynamics we face are the products of ever-evolving global economic and political systems set up to exploit those living on the margins. Despite centuries of Black freedom struggle in the Americas we continue to fall short of getting free. Our people's history of resistance is not fully known or valued—despite serving as a model for liberation struggles throughout the world. *Knowledge must be democratized.* Principled debate and struggle distributes knowledge and generates ideas. And in doing so, people can have radical visions of their very own. Political discomfort is necessary for growth.

We are resilient and refuse to stop believing in the possibility of a world where we live in dignity. We don't just imagine it, we can *feel* it, even when we don't see it coming to pass in our own lifetime. Our imagination lives despite messages and actions telling us that we are not good enough, human enough, or woman enough. And we *do* think that is possible in our lifetime, here, right now. It is possible *right now.* The ability for us to live and walk down the street without being afraid of being physically, sexually, or mentally assaulted is possible. It's possible for our children to have radical imaginations. It's possible for our children to engage in a science experiment and not end up in handcuffs as sixteen-year-old Kiera Wilmot did in 2013 in Florida, as too many of our children have. And it's important to realize that even if we don't live to see the change we envision, contributing to the process is necessary. Imagine that there are buckets and that one of those really big water towers has to be filled. Each of us, and I mean each of us, has a contribution to make toward filling it. Everyone has a role, and no one person can begin to do it all. Malcolm X is not coming back to save us. There is no Dr. King, and there is no Ella Baker. There is no single charismatic leader or organizer coming to save us or to free us. But it is collectively possible to liberate ourselves and continue the permanent project toward enabling human dignity.

At the same time, today's movement is in a repeating cycle of fighting the same battles fought by our ancestors, because we are often looking at incomplete models, theories, and histories. There are far too many incomplete stories and partial solutions to getting free. We must look back to where we came from to help determine where we must go.

CHAPTER 3

THE CASE FOR REIMAGINING THE BLACK RADICAL TRADITION

Men make their own history, but they do not make it just as they please; they do not make it under circumstances directly encoun-tered, given and transmitted from the past.

—KARL MARX, *The Eighteenth Brumaire of Louis Bonaparte*

I fell in love with history a long time ago. Books and documenta-ries were an escape to a different world. In books I could visit differ-ent periods of time and different cultures and at times connect with characters as if they were just like me. I found history in fiction and nonfiction books. I saw myself in Toni Morrison's telling of Pecola Breedlove's struggle with sexual violence, poverty, and identity in *The Bluest Eye.* I knew what it felt like to stand in a mirror and wish I were a little white girl. I saw myself in April Sinclair's *Coffee Will Make You Black,* and the coming-of-age story of a Black lesbian was closer to home than I was willing to accept as a teenager. I watched *Eyes on the Prize* and *Watermelon Woman.* I devoured tales about Black life, and at times the world they took me to was as bleak as the one I was afraid to live in. I didn't realize it at the time, but in my escape to other places I was searching for meaning and belonging. Since then, I've continued to cultivate my seemingly insatiable appetite for knowledge. I constantly feel behind my peers who studied Black radicalism and feminist and queer theory in school and on their own. I never feel as well-read as I should be. Though I always had access to books, much of what I was exposed to was incomplete and fell short somehow. Many of the texts and sources treated as essential didn't go far enough. I found myself asking, "Well, what came before capitalism? Didn't patriarchy exist?" Or, "Where are the women in this story? Where are the queer folks?"

I have been crafting more complete stories about Black people and our movements for Black liberation for a long time. I am now clear that my hunger for a more complete story must become a shared strategy for collective liberation. The incalculable amounts of agents for Black liberation are, and were, more robust than the often single story of charisma, strength, and strategies I learned as a student.

Incomplete stories about the history of the struggle for Black liberation have led to ineffective solutions for our collective liberation. If the relationship between two people is one of the smallest units of movement building, then the stories we hear and share within those relationships are the springboards for action. Stories provide context, can describe and explain strategy, and can help people understand what happens in the world. People process stories and make choices based on what they conclude.

Activists leverage stories to explain complex ideas. People connect to stories easier than they connect with sheer facts. Numbers become numbing. Tables and charts don't usually strike us as viscerally as stories do. And while there are so many dominant forces affirming that facts simply don't matter, stories do. Stories draw out emotions. They allow us to see, taste, and feel moments. If the stories we tell about Black people's experiences of resistance and resilience are incomplete, our movements to transform them, to enact them, will be insufficient and ineffective.

Anti-Blackness limits expertise to people who are not invested in collective liberation. Anti-Blackness says that intellectualism is not the realm of everyday Black folks. Instead it advances the idea that Black radicals who do intellectual work are not truly radical or contributing to collective liberation. Therefore it is our duty to be rigorous and to collectivize the keeping and sharing of our own stories. Our movement needs griots, using multiple mediums, to clarify and expand the stories of the Black radical tradition.

Today's Black activists play a dangerous game with history. On the one hand, activists look back at the Black freedom struggles of the past with deep nostalgia. On the other hand, the same people identify problems and critique what happened before us without context or grounding. Activists love and hate the civil rights movement and its best-known strategies. We groan at the idea of "another march" but will call for mass mobilizations in the aftermath of the killing of one of our own. We romanticize the Black Power movement while questioning the role and significance of Black women and queer leaders. This game, just like our lives, is full of contradictions. These contradictions should, however, be recognized and not contribute to a collective amnesia regarding Black movement history. We can hold all those truths in order to make more informed and strategic decisions as a movement.

Contemporary historians work diligently to uncover stories of leaders like Ella Baker, Rosa Parks, and Bayard Rustin. It is not uncommon for someone to insert a "well, actually, Rosa Parks wasn't just tired" or an "Ella Baker is underrated" or a "Bayard Rustin wasn't allowed to speak at the March on Washington because he was gay." Most of us know which March on Washington I'm talking about because, for all intents and purposes, the 1963 march is the only one in the history of social movements that takes up so much significance and space. We love and hate to dig into histories. As Black people, there's so much to love and hate from our histories. Regardless, they are ours. Acknowledging and wrestling with all they entail not only advance our knowledge; they also give us the juice we need to secure our collective liberation.

It is counterrevolutionary to tell stories about the Black radical tradition that fail to offer critiques, lessons, and insights about how white supremacy breeds systems of gender and sexual oppression. The story of white supremacy is inherently one of gender and sexual violence. Analysis of patriarchal violence is not an adjunct but a cornerstone for understanding why Black liberation is necessary. If a more holistic history of the Black radical tradition were valued, then the movement strategies and tactics would be more radical and relevant to all Black people. We not only leave stories on the table, unexamined, when the radical work of Black feminist and queer liberation is undervalued, we also disdain effective strategy and tactics. Our people can't afford for us to leave any of our genius on the table.

What I know for sure is that stories of injustice motivate people to take action. The story of seventeen-year-old Trayvon Martin's slaying by a self-appointed vigilante in 2012 led to mass mobilizations and a month-long occupation of the Florida state legislature led by Power U and the Dream Defenders. The August 9, 2014, killing of Mike Brown and attacks on young Black people honoring his life mobilized people in Ferguson, Missouri, and around the world. Outrage from the acquittal of the Chicago police officer who killed twenty-one-year-old Rekia Boyd on March 21, 2012, launched a national day of direct action involving over fifteen US cities and calling for an end to state-sanctioned violence against all Black women, girls, and femmes.

What would be possible if we told more complete stories about the Black radical tradition? What would be possible if the stories of Black radical tradition were created by using a Black queer feminist lens? Understandings of the Black radical tradition would be more complete, and our movement would better understand how to craft effective liberatory strategies for all. Take, for example, the story of Recy Taylor and the international movement her bravery sparked. In 1944, the young mother was kidnapped and raped by a group of young white men and boys in Abbeville, Alabama. Her decision to tell her story motivated activists, Black soldiers in World War II, and journalists across the world to take on sexual violence against Black women as a civil rights and international human rights issue. Taylor's story was among many interventions across the US to end white men's sexual terrorism against Black women and girls. As Danielle McGuire writes in *At the Dark End of the Street: Black Women, Rape, and Resistance*, to understand the impact of sexual terrorism on the lives of Black folks and "within the larger freedom struggle, we have to interpret, if not rewrite, the history of the civil rights movement."[1]

Rosa Parks, an experienced activist, leader, and Alabama native, returned to her childhood home, Abbeville, to investigate the rape, heard Taylor's story, and began to organize. Parks secured and leveraged the support of influential Black Alabama leaders, including the head of the Alabama Brotherhood of Sleeping Car Porters, E. D. Nixon, to form the Alabama Committee for Equal Justice for Mrs. Recy Taylor. The *Chicago Defender* called the committee's efforts the "strongest campaign for equal justice to be seen in a decade."[2] The campaign built an unprecedented united front against the rape of Black women and girls. Union leaders joined YWCA, NAACP, and Communist Party leaders to call for justice for Taylor. An emergency meeting in New York City brought "Queen Mother" Audley Moore, an experienced Black nationalist and anti-rape activist, into the campaign. Black communists and leftist newspapers also joined the cause. This united front raised funds, led a local investigation of the attack in Abbeville, and directed demands for justice to Alabama governor Chauncey Sparks. It was a key effort in the struggle for Black liberation. Yet this work—led by Black women and supported nationally by Black labor leaders, media, and organizations—is not widely known in the popular history of the civil rights movement as told in the renowned television documentary series *Eyes on the Prize*, much less in high school history textbooks.

———

If the Alabama Committee for Equal Justice for Mrs. Recy Taylor were to be widely valued as a critical national and international human rights campaign, today's activists would have more models of how to build effective international campaigns that address present-day racism and gendered injustice. We might, for example, leverage the power of Black soldiers and veterans. The campaign for justice for Recy Taylor was waged during a global fight against fascist regimes in Germany and Italy. McGuire notes that the editorial director of the *Army News* warned Governor Sparks that if the pamphlet detailing the gang rape of Mrs. Taylor "reaches any considerable number of Negro soldiers in our armed services, and I have no doubt it will, it will greatly affect their efficiency. . . . This of course will be very bad for war effort, for it is senseless to fight fascism abroad if fascistic influences are to be protected at home.[3] We should also consider what it means to run campaigns centered on the story of an individual without leaving the person behind. That's what happened to Recy Taylor. The campaign went beyond her and took on a new life with little regard for her well-being or security. If this story was valued, perhaps we would be collectively concerned about the safety of young Black women leaders who live with daily threats of violence and harassment for daring to uplift ourselves, as well as LGBTQ folks, while also uplifting Black men and boys; I would personally appreciate that.

What would have been possible if Bayard Rustin's work as an architect of the 1963 March on Washington for Jobs and Justice had been acclaimed long before he received the Presidential Medal of Freedom in 2013, years after his death? What would young people during the 1970s, 1980s, and 1990s have thought possible? Instead Rustin, an openly gay Black man, was for a long time left in the shadows of more palatable leaders. Some of the slight has begun to be addressed. The Human Rights Campaign, a highly corporate and liberal LGBTQ rights organization, placed a large banner with Rustin's image on it in front of its headquarters for a while. But Rustin's strategic thinking and life work have yet to be widely studied and understood.

Rustin and Malcolm X had a riveting public debate about nationalism and integration, and we ought to know about this. Their debate and disagreements are like those we continue to have today. Where did the two titans converge, and where did they diverge? Rustin had been arrested twenty-two times for various acts of civil disobedience and Malcolm X had spent years in prison by the time they met and discussed the Black freedom struggle. There is much to learn from their brief exchange, and there is much to try to reconcile. The clashes of Malcolm X and Martin Luther King Jr. are meanwhile well-known. We still contend with questions of nationalism (be it land-based or purely social) in our movement today. Black children attend segregated schools just as they did before *Brown v. Board of Education*. The promise of integration—for better health and education, safety, and justice for all Black people—has not been fulfilled. And homophobia still hinders understanding and thwarts liberation.

What would be possible if Black children were taught that Marsha P. Johnson and Sylvia Rivera were among the founders of the LGBTQ rights movement in the United States? Johnson and Rivera cofounded the world's first-known trans rights organization, Street Transvestite Action Revolutionaries (STAR). Johnson, a legend for some, should be elevated within the Black radical tradition. White gay politician Harvey Milk is now iconic, but what if there were multimillion-dollar-budget feature films about Marsha Johnson made by Black trans women like Reina Gossett, who has dedicated her life to telling her story? What if young people who learned Johnson's story came to see themselves as rebels who could spark an entire movement? How could that help to dismantle transphobia and the violence that transgender women and gender-nonconforming people experience? Marsha P. Johnson and people like her are not only kept out of the collective memory of the Black radical tradition but are also marginalized within the mainstream gay rights community, the LGBTQ movement, today. The emergence of the Trans Women of Color Collective, in Ohio, founded by Black trans women including Elle Hearns, should be much more integral to our telling of today's Black liberation movement. If our children are able to digest the historical truths of Black slavery and lynching, they can also digest the historical truths about the role of Black transgender folks in fighting for our collective liberation.

What if the history of the Black feminist movement were to be taught alongside that of the civil rights movement? As Kimberly Springer argues, Black women were "the first activists in the United States to theorize and act upon the intersections of race, gender, and class."[4] These were enslaved women, the formerly enslaved, and descendants of enslaved Africans. They were the women who marched at the back of the 1913 women's suffrage march on Washington and those who exposed the horrors of lynching and sexual violence against Black women and girls across the United States. Black women activists could not come to the table as the popular class known as "race men" did. As "race women," gender was inseparable from their work and vision for liberation (as was class). This work epitomizes the Black radical tradition, yet it is largely missing from popular stories about Black resistance.

I am not suggesting that we add Black women and LGBTQ folks to the Black History Month celebration so that people simply know more facts. I'm also not suggesting that we get rid of the stories told most often. I am arguing that those organizing political education programs reimagine what is essential and foundational. Black radical feminism should be considered basic, not something advanced or optional. If organizers and educators are committed enough to dig into complex theories on racial capitalism, white supremacy, and anti-Blackness, then they can also commit to digging into patriarchy, homophobia, and transphobia. If Black people experience any type of systemic oppression and have taken up the duty to resist it, then we organizers have the duty to centralize radical Black queer and feminist work in our political education. The story of the Black Left should include these histories, as well as the stories of the labor, communist, socialist, LGBTQ, and gender justice movements.

Radical Black queer and feminist work is largely marginalized, but that does not diminish its significance and strategic imperative today. Our forebears and contemporary vanguards deserve respect and acknowledgement followed by action.

Patriarchy and its offspring, homophobia and transphobia, have no place in our movement. To allow these to go unchecked is counterrevolutionary. If your liberation movement has people on the sidelines (or absent altogether), then it's not really liberatory. As my good friend and comrade Hiram Rivera says, "Colonized minds do colonized things." None of us are immune to the effects of white supremacy, capitalism, anti-Blackness, and patriarchal systems.

One could argue that people can only teach what they know. Or, looking at it from a different perspective, at some point we all lack knowledge about something until we choose or are forced to learn. Anyone committed to collective liberation must acknowledge ignorance and take up the work of comprehensive political education. For example, I have been out of my depth on disability justice and climate change, to name two topics, and so I follow the lead of people who are more knowledgeable. But this doesn't let me off the hook: I still need to seek out knowledge on my own about these issues.

Organizers have to believe that Black people, no matter their level of formal education, can understand complex ideas and apply them to real life. I recall hearing a Black man in my neighborhood sum up racial capitalism in a single sentence, and it always stuck with me. I was driving home with two comrades, and as we turned the corner we saw a Black person lying on the ground. This person was surrounded by a small group of people, and an ambulance was pulling up. A man had been shot, and it had happened just up the block from where I live, in a neighborhood that is hyper-surveilled by the police. There are constantly cop cars driving around and parked at intersections. This particular spot, near a train station, always has at least one cop car nearby. I parked, and we walked to the site of the shooting. I stood next to a middle-aged Black man who reminded me of most of the men in my family. Maybe I seemed familiar to him, too, because he started talking. "The police are out here every day," he observed, "and they're only here to protect these stores, this property, not the people." That moment reinforced my belief that everyday Black folks understand what's going on. The challenge is to harness this understanding for collective use. Knowledge and understanding come first, but how can we use them to inform movements? Black folks can do both: not just understand but also act.

How do we do it? First, developing individual and collective commitment to advance a movement requires more than information. It takes the cultivation of knowledge in fields of study that people can relate to. All people concerned with collective liberation have the duty to pursue knowledge, and today's movement for Black liberation must cultivate knowledge in every facet of our work. And we must also see every act, every engagement, as an opportunity to learn or to teach or both. The exchange of stories in everyday conversations and through social media is insufficient. Our demands for systemic change must get at the root of how Black people receive knowledge and what knowledge we receive. The work of dismantling the school-to-prison pipeline entails understanding, critiquing, and reshaping what our children are being taught.

There are barriers to our gaining knowledge that advances our struggle, but we have a duty to break down the barriers. One way is by fostering a more holistic telling of the Black radical tradition. The need for researching, documenting, writing, filming, and just telling our stories is urgent. There are imaginations to liberate and liberated imaginations to inspire and aid. As with opinions, not all books or documentary resources are good. Consumers of information must ask, "Who's the focus of this story? Who's marginalized or left out? Who is depicted as good and who as bad?" The decision to swallow or spit out what we chew requires rigor. Future generations (including children today) will be influenced by our choices.

Fortunately, much of this work has already been done. Black people have done the work of explaining the impact of systemic types of oppression on our lives. Someone has written, created visual art, developed policy, sung songs, and even danced to explain visions for collective liberation. As activists and organizers, it is our duty to create and to keep investigating new information to be transformed into knowledge. While it is possible for someone from outside of a community to tell its history, why not invest in people who come from a community and the people who have made the history to tell it? That would require the breaking down of social and economic hierarchies that validate the expertise of some over others. Community-controlled and community-owned history projects, art installations, oral history, photography archives, and related projects should be an important part of our movement. Knowledge of what our people have been through is powerful. It allows us to demand more and know that change is not only needed, it is inevitable. The question is: what kind of change do we wish to see?

Learning is an ongoing project. Our movement has a duty to move marginalized histories to the center of the Black radical tradition.

LET'S NOT DEAL WITH RACE FIRST

Stories help make sense of the past, present, and future. The stories we learn as children inform how we see the world as adults. Not everyone is fortunate enough to be in an environment where critical thinking is the standard, so many of those stories are accepted without questioning them. The dominant stories about Black liberation often leave out significant women, LGBTQ folks, and people from across the African diaspora outside the United States. Entire organizations and communities are left out of dominant Black movement histories too.

Just as we cannot encompass all of what it means to be Black in one neat story, we cannot fit Black feminist activism into a single story or movement. Blackness and Black feminist activism are so deep and wide that it would be impossible to fit them into a single narrative. Scholar and philosopher Joy James criticizes "the 'framing' of feminism in ways that either erase the contributions of radical Black women or depict a homogenous Black feminism as an (corrective or rebellious) appendage to either anti-racist or feminist struggles."[5] Still, they deserve to be at the forefront, not for the sake of inclusivity alone, but because radical Black feminist visions are often more complete, more honest, more revolutionary than what is allowed to be considered important or essential.

Black feminists and LGBTQ activists are often told that they are "hijacking," being "divisive," "co-opting," or simply distracting from what is more important. This silencing is propped up by the running currents of patriarchy and misogyny and by the absence of the converging and diverging Black feminist and LGBTQ liberation movements in dominant stories about social movements in the United States and the broader African diaspora. Our ancestors, elders, and comrades deserve more than that. Radical Black feminists and LGBTQ leaders have historically challenged not just white supremacy but also capitalism, patriarchy, transphobia, heterosexism, and homophobia sometimes inside of Black movement spaces—and they have been marginalized for this.

I want the lie that Black people cannot be Black, queer, trans, and women at the same time to die a swift death. I want that lie to die alongside the idea that any one group of Black people is inherently more worthy to be free than any other. All types of Black people are in cages, but many receive little attention and support. Even with the near impossibility of respectability politics to benefit incarcerated people, some imprisoned Black people are still perceived as worthier of our empathy than others. At the same time, someone had to organize and tell stories of imprisonment—most importantly the stories of those who have been or are incarcerated—in order for today's prison abolition movement to even exist. Now is the time for our generation to make a coordinated push, to go beyond what is comfortable, and to value all types of stories. The stories of the sex worker, for example, need telling. To shine a light on jailed sex workers would expose so many systems of oppression. Our campaign to end mass incarceration ought to target economic justice and publicize their stories.

Black activists must be willing to have frank conversations at times when it feels like everything is on the line. I say this from firsthand experience. During the Baltimore uprising I found myself talking with a member of a notorious street organization about the role of women in the movement. He towered over my five-foot-two frame, so I had to look up at the brother the whole time. It must have been a curious sight for anyone who was paying attention. The brother insisted that Black women shouldn't be out in the streets fighting and that it was the Black man's role. He insisted this while surrounded by hundreds of Black women on the street during the day's mass mobilization. We went back and forth for a few minutes, and I didn't completely change his mind, but there were moments of agreement. Having those conversations is about more than letting go of fear or respectability. Doing that work is about valuing our people enough to believe that we can be transformed.

People who need examples for why patriarchy is counterrevolutionary can look to Burkina Faso's former president Thomas Sankara and the people who led the 1983 revolution in Burkina Faso. They understood that a revolution that didn't prioritize dismantling patriarchy was no revolution at all. In "The Revolution Cannot Triumph without the Emancipation of Women," Sankara's 1987 speech commemorating International Women's Day, he said:

> Posing the question of women in Burkinabé society today means posing the abolition of the system of slavery to which they have been subjected for millennia. The first step is to try to understand how this system works, to grasp its real nature in all its subtlety, in order then to work out a line of action that can lead to women's total emancipation. In other words, in order to win this battle that men and women have in common, we must be familiar with all aspects of the woman question on a world scale and here in Burkina. We must understand how the struggle of the Burkinabé woman is part of a worldwide struggle of all women and, beyond that, part of the struggle for the full rehabilitation of our continent. Thus, women's emancipation is at the heart of the question of humanity itself, here and everywhere. The question is thus universal in character.[6]

These words were not mere lip service. Sankara and the revolutionary forces took action to form several women's initiatives. Sankara and the other leaders of the Burkinabé independence movement emphasized self-determination and self-reliance as a part of a project to repair what was broken by the destruction of colonialism. Sankara understood that dismantling patriarchy was intrinsically tied to dismantling the oppression of his people. One could not happen without the other. If the Black radical tradition focused on Sankara as a revolutionary leader, there would be several lessons to learn. He and the Burkinabé movement's other leaders worked not only to decolonize the land and the economy but also to decolonize their people's minds. And Sankara was assassinated for that. That's how dangerous his ideas and the movement's efforts were to colonial powers and interests.

Black people are not a monolith. The threads that make up our collective experiences on earth are so long that they could be woven into a fabric that would cover the earth. Our stories are not uniform and neither are our politics. Stories that paint Black people as a monolith reduce the depth of our humanity and prevent us from building movements that address all systems of oppression. Yet even today Black activists are encouraged by people with limited imaginations to put race first—which more often than not means to consider *only* race, not class, gender, or sexuality. But our struggle does not need to be monolithic in order to be successful. White supremacy and capitalism teach us to believe in a scarcity of space. The "crooked room" described by scholar Melissa Harris-Perry, the one in which Black women are quarantined, exists in a larger house that Black people inhabit.[7] Limiting the understanding of who Black people are, what we've endured, and where we must go is not only counterproductive, it will not stop us from being killed. In the struggle for Black liberation, there should be no hierarchy of issues worth fighting for. However, in almost every sector of our movement, the voiceless and powerless struggle for room in a world dominated by systems that oppress us and people who don't want us to be free.

Views of liberal white folks help perpetuate this problem. Activist communities claiming to be progressive and radical recycle incomplete stories about movement history, lionizing Martin Luther King Jr.'s most well-known views while ignoring his stance for reproductive rights and radicalization in his later years. The monolithic view of history is evident in every mural containing an image of Marcus Garvey but not Amy Jacques Garvey. Likewise witness Christopher Street Park in New York City where the Stonewall Rebellion is commemorated without any mention of Marsha P. Johnson or her comrade Sylvia Rivera. Histories are centered on the people who make them. When arbiters of knowledge (e.g., educators, intellectuals, and historians) fail to value and tell the histories of significant strategists and leaders, we miss their vision, and perhaps the foundation they built crumbles a bit instead of being maintained.

If we told a more complete story of the Black radical tradition, one that grounds itself in the stories of Black feminist, queer, and trans liberation work, we would have more complete and effective solutions for the problems we encounter: what to do in moments of crisis and outrage, how to talk about fascism with everyday people, how to organize people with little access to resources, and how to oppose groups that use political and economic power to oppress.

IT IS OUR DUTY TO RECLAIM OUR MEMORIES AND KNOWLEDGE

I wince every time I hear someone exclaim that "young people just don't know their history." This assertion almost always indicates lack of understanding. We *are* our history, and we know how important it is. But the transatlantic slave trade, hundreds of years of slavery, and systemic barriers to formal education greatly diminished Black folks' ability to hold on to their histories, culture, traditions, and religion. For over three hundred years, the majority of Black people living in the United States could not freely record or access their history. Today we have access to information and knowledge our ancestors never had. It would be disrespectful of me to expect enslaved Africans to carry all of our peoples' history across the Atlantic Ocean.

It is important to ask: Who is responsible for educating young people? Who influences the information children receive? What have been the barriers to young people learning histories of resistance?

Our ancestors faced systemic violence for their efforts to hold on to their culture. While it is no longer forbidden for Black people to read, access to quality education has never been guaranteed for Black children in the US Our people have always had to fight for it, and we continue to fight today. Anti-Blackness is adaptable in the face of resistance to oppression, the systems and people who uphold it are backed by power structures ensuring that oppression is the status quo, and quality education is a privilege when it should be a right.

Children across the United States spend most of their waking hours in school. What are they learning? What is seen as valuable knowledge? Some parents choose to start their own schools, send their children to private schools, or home-school their children. Those efforts are necessary, and so are efforts to address the educational needs of students who have no access to these alternatives to public schools. Educational work should be central in our organizing efforts.

All activists and organizers would benefit by learning from Black LGBTQ and feminist movements, by prioritizing their study. There is so much to gain from the illuminating words of Toni Morrison, bell hooks, Bruce Nugent, Audre Lorde, Joseph Beam, Angela Davis, Alice Walker, Essex Hemphill, and Lorraine Hansberry. The hyper-visibility of Black women, lesbian, gay, bisexual, transgender, and queer leaders in today's struggle for Black liberation is not by happenstance. We were conjured up through generations of magic. And, as in almost every childhood story or horror film you've seen, magic performed by women and outsiders is considered suspicious and dangerous and targeted with violence.

I exist, and I am able to lead unapologetically because of the generations of Black feminist, prisoner-rights, transgender, gay, dyke, lesbian, and queer resistance that came before me. My history is that of rebels, revolutionaries, and Maroons, from the transatlantic slave through the civil rights and Black Power movements, the Compton's Cafeteria riot, and the Stonewall Rebellion.[8] These examples of resistance illustrate the power of people who have come together based on shared experiences, cultures, and visions for what is possible. The intellectual labor, community organizing, and cultural labor of our ancestors and elders laid the groundwork for activists from all backgrounds today and help us understand collective liberation. Their freedom-dreaming resulted in the building of movements that fought for the eradication of racism, sexism, transphobia, and homophobia.

The words "intersectionality," "queer," "anti-racist," and "anticapitalist" roll off the tongues of so many radical Black activists. No one learns those words and what they mean on their own. Black feminists, Ballroom legends, queer folks, and people who fit no binaries have done the groundwork but are taken for granted in far too many movement spaces to this day. What is common terminology and practice in social justice circles today was theorized, written about, organized around, and fought for by people whose names we may never know.

What we include in the story of the Black radical tradition must account for these forebears without apology. The Black radical tradition includes writing and rewriting the history of our people. Let us all accept that responsibility. Record your own stories. Protect your family's history. Knowing these stories is important for collective liberation. It is not the responsibility of any one person to hold all the knowledge, of course. Instead, each of us has the duty to honor our present and past, while encouraging future generations to take up the work when it's their turn. Cultivating, keeping, and sharing knowledge is labor and must be valued as such.

Black people are no strangers to having to tell our own histories. We are familiar with the media and historians telling stories that are either false or completely erase our contributions. Black scholars like John Hope Franklin, Mary Frances Berry, Manning Marable, and Cheikh Anta Diop created great histories of Black people meant to tell truths that white male historians failed to tell. At the same time, radical Black cultural workers, educators, and activists have had to do the same work—to tell more-complete stories about Black history that don't simply add women and LGBTQ folks but that center us. Those who benefit from our oppression will not do that work. Those of us committed to collective liberation must do it, and then, after the work of keeping and sharing these stories, we must take effective action toward collective liberation.

CHAPTER 4

THREE COMMITMENTS

We are each other's business;
we are each other's harvest;
we are each other's magnitude and bond.

—GWENDOLYN BROOKS

Home is anywhere we belong, where we grow, where we're challenged, and where we're in relationship with others. BYP100 is my first political home. As a founding member of the organization, I've helped shape it, shared countless meals with fellow members, and crafted plans for how we could improve it and improve the Black liberation movement. This political home isn't based in one location. Like many Black people, we move. My political home is where I develop as a leader, where I belong with people who share values and vision and who take action for collective liberation.

Movement building is spiritual work. It is beyond audacious to build an organization unlike one any of us has ever been a part of—one based on group leadership and where marginalized people are centered. If someone had traveled to the future and compiled a list of things we accomplished in our first year, then brought it to us in 2013, at our start, we would have all exclaimed, "Hell, no!" We had extremely limited resources in the first year, and I was the only full-time paid staff member for two years. The majority of our leadership worked without pay or with modest pay. Money was tight, and I slept on members' couches and figured out how to make ten dollars out of fifty cents. A handful of folks who carried major areas of our work daily did so without pay.

BYP100 possessed a level of grit at the beginning that Black folks are used to dealing with. Our team worked hard to build an infrastructure that could last, that could stand up to the test of the work set before us. In the early days, people such as Jasson Perez, Jessica Pierce, Terrance Laney, Rose Afriyie, Jonathan Lykes, and many others helped build the organization locally and nationally. Even with foresight, research, and decades of collective experience, we were not prepared for the challenges and pain to come. We had many breakdowns, and along the way I learned that we weren't unique in our struggles. Not only were we repeating experiences of previous movements before our time; we were experiencing the same challenges as similar organizations that also emerged during this era of the Black liberation movement, including the Black Lives Matter Global Network and the Dream Defenders. The patterns of what builds up and breaks down organizations reflect broader movement forces and social realities.

Based on my experience and research of social movements, I have found that atrophy or breakdowns within movements for Black liberation, historically and in the present, largely derive from people not seeing themselves in the work, being traumatized, and not giving themselves—or not being allowed—time and space to do ongoing self-work and healing. Another factor is a culture of liberalism that allows for unchecked conflict and unprincipled struggle.

There are three collective commitments our movements must take up to regenerate:

1. Building many strong leaders
2. Adopting healing justice as a core organizing value and practice
3. Combating liberalism with principled struggle

One way to understand these dynamics is by placing them into a helpful framework that I learned from teacher and comrade Sendolo Diaminah. Sendolo taught me to categorize challenges into three groups: nuisances, problems, and dilemmas. Nuisances are challenges (from people or situations) that are annoying yet tolerable. Problems are challenges that can be solved. Dilemmas are challenges that have to be navigated but seem unresolvable. These categories seem distinct, but they are connected, and they exist not only inside our organizations but also between allies.

Of course, challenges are part of life, and they force us to make choices about what to do and how to show up. Our choices can be coerced or not. The challenges we encounter and the available resources we have to deal with them inevitably depend on who we are. In movement work, our challenges can feel like matters of life and death. Sometimes they actually are matters of life and death. In facing them, we feel urgency, anxiety, and pressure—and this can help build a movement, but it can also break one down. As humans who have survived generations of trauma, Black folks are resilient but also vulnerable to pain. We can and do show up to movement spaces holding all of that trauma in our minds and that pain in our bodies.

A social movement is in many ways like a human body. The body is made up of cells that naturally die and regenerate, whether or not people eat healthful diets, exercise, take pharmaceuticals, and meditate. Regardless of action or inaction, beyond our control cells atrophy and die. And sometimes this destruction is aided by outside sources. Toxic chemicals, negligently distributed into our environments by corporations, can cause cancer. Likewise people suffer and sometimes die when others commit acts of violence. There are things that we knowingly put into our bodies, things that go into our bodies without our consent, and things that we do with our bodies that make them more or less healthy. We feel and we think with these bodies we have, bodies of different shapes, sizes, and abilities.

Our bodies and what we experience in them are inextricably connected to movements we join. And there are entire industries that profit from commodifying everything that involves the body, including pleasure, forced and exploitative labor, and so-called miracle methods to treat whatever ails us. Someone always wins, and it is usually not the laborer or the consumer.

People take action when they get tired of being on the losing side. In the US, the losing side is not only the 99 percent; there are levels of marginalization and oppression. People within the 99 percent often act against the interests of people who have just as much wealth—or much less. Social movements emerge when people decide that change is necessary and take collective action over a period of time toward achieving a set of goals. Examples include the Occupy Movement, the Fight for 15, and ongoing land-based struggles in the US and around the world.

In any social movement there are dynamics that build up and regenerate it and dynamics that undermine it. Understanding what builds up and what breaks down our movements and its smaller parts is crucial to our developing an effective strategy and winning. No one person or organization can create an antidote to the various things that break our movements down. The breakdowns, if thoroughly assessed, should be springboards for transforming our work.

BUILD STRONG LEADERS

Community organizing toward liberation requires people in ongoing and substantive public relationships with each other, people with shared interests, to work toward shared goals. When people have no stake in the work, they not only lose interest but can also be prone to marginalizing those with whom they claim to be in struggle. I advise young organizers to be wary about claims of selflessness regarding the shared work. Selflessness is problematic because it is devoid of someone's vision for the world and their place in it. Self-interest, on the other hand, situates you, your vision, and your values in relationship with others. Identifying self-interest is essential because it allows individuals to work not simply as allies but as accomplices in our collective liberation. Knowing one's self-interest can be the difference between staying home and attending a weekly organizing meeting. Interrogating self-interest allows us to identify what's at stake for ourselves, even when we are not the most directly impacted. What is your self-interest?

I stay in my work because I am the daughter of a woman who continues to work a low-wage job despite years of experience that should have resulted in much more than a basic income. I stay in this work because I grew up in a household where heat during Chicago winters was not always guaranteed. People should not have to live without heat in a country where renewable, affordable energy is possible. I stay in this work because I fear that I could one day be a Black woman pulled over in her car for failing to signal and later found dead in a jail cell. Sandra Bland lost her life that way. I am afraid that I could too.

What is at stake for me in striving to end violent death for Black people? I am not a Black man, boy, or trans woman, but we share a common heritage through our shared oppressors. We all inherited a world where our bodies are marked for exploitation and violent death, and we are connected through our struggles and the genius of our people. That genius fights for our lives. That genius brings us together to mourn and to celebrate. That genius set forth radical visions for Black liberation long before we were born. The genius may not have had knowledge of what our lives would be like today, but it created necessary openings for people to create change and transformation.

Everyone interested in personal or collective pursuits for liberation must look into themselves to investigate why they come into this work. Is it because you want your children to grow up in a world different from the one you inherited? That you want to walk down streets where no one is harassed because of their perceived or actual gender identity? Because you understand that the destruction of poor communities miles away from your comfortable home is just an economic recession away from your own front door? Or is it simply because you see the humanity in other people despite what you've been told? All people *must* see themselves in the work and have something at stake.

Once we recognize our self-interest, we also have to humble ourselves to understand that what is at stake for us may not be pressing for others. Black pain and violent death are center stage in kitchen table conversations and the media. Videos of a Black girl being thrown to the ground in her swimsuit, Walter Scott being gunned down while running away, and an art exhibit depicting Mike Brown's murdered body are accessible to millions. Many Black folks are walking around in perpetual states of trauma. Murders of Black trans women are coming into the consciousness of more people, despite years of people resisting this violent trend. People whose lives are at stake must see themselves in the work of liberation movements that are effective and have resources or they will rightfully stay away. And if marginalized people are not in the movement to offer critical analysis and perspective, our movement will not succeed.

If you are not among the marginalized or at risk of violence, then what are you best positioned to do? All leaders must ask themselves: what work needs to be done, what am I being asked to do, and what am I best positioned to do? Leaders do not get to do what they want at all times, and various roles must be filled whether we like it or not.

Just as you have to see yourself in the work, you have to be able to lead it. The analogy of passing the torch, while popular, isn't useful, and I recall an elder telling me that there was no torch to pass. In other words, folks should not have to ask for permission to organize with their own people. Waiting for permission to take action and lead serves only those who wish to maintain power over people.

As Frederick Douglass observed in his "West India Emancipation" speech, "power concedes nothing without demand." And demands are most powerful when made collectively.

Consent is necessary, however, from those we organize in our communities, from the beginning to the end of any strategy, and it is crucial to make room for other people to lead and learn—and to give them space to make mistakes. Acting alone or with a small group only serves one or a few, and we need to foster more leaders to insure that our work will continue. We must build and grow with one another. And our failures, affecting us as a collective, should provide opportunities for growth and learning.

To counter the weakening effects of people not seeing themselves in the work, organizations and the movement at large must invest in leadership development. It makes individuals and the collective stronger. People don't come into movement work with fully baked analyses and strategies. Jeremy Tyler, when he was a new BYP100 member, said, "I might not be all the way woke, but I'm not asleep anymore." What would be possible if more of us came to the work in that way? What would be possible if we gave ourselves and others room to grow? Since we are always in a state of emergency, our movement requires this.

Organizations should focus on developing as many leaders as possible who are able to analyze critically and have solid organizing skills. This does not mean that everyone will be or has to be a full-time organizer. What it does mean is that more and more people will be equipped to develop and move projects, campaigns, and programs forward. It takes many leaders to raise and sustain a movement beyond a moment: strategic communicators, child-care workers, people who can cook for large groups, people to grow food, health practitioners, and many more. A community organizer's skill should be measured in how many leaders one helps develop, not in how many campaign victories one claims.

It takes time to digest the reality of the world we live in and make sense of how we are situated in the broader human experience. It takes time to understand our individual roles in building collective power. It takes time to see how our talents, gifts, and skills can contribute to the work. It also takes time to decide whether something is worth an investment of our time and money.

When people see that they matter in organizing spaces, they are more likely to repeatedly show up. It takes time to engage individuals in the process of building relationships in the movement, but it is more than worth it. In building those relationships, we are better able as organizers and leaders to ascertain what brings people to the table and what may keep them there, especially if we see that they have something important, large or small, enabling our work. Good movement organizing recognizes this by holding one-on-one or relational meetings, house meetings, and study groups.

People often misread Ella Baker's declaration that "strong people don't need strong leaders" as a statement against leadership. Instead she was cautioning movements against valorizing single charismatic leaders, especially ones not grounded in or accountable to communities. She understood that transformative change requires the leadership of many people. The wisdom was shared in a time when individual Black men were seen—by media and national decision-makers—as the most essential leaders in the civil rights movement. Baker saw the failures of building around personalities and individual leaders instead of building around the needs of the people and developing many leaders to move the work forward.

Leaders do initiate and drive movement building, but, as Baker asserted, "Martin [Luther King Jr.] didn't make the movement, the movement made Martin." King was an exceptional leader, but still it took countless leaders and countless people on the ground to create what we reflect back on as one of the greatest social movements ever. Yes, he was charismatic. But charismatic leaders who fail to build relationships and foster more leaders are setting themselves up for martyrdom, and their work may grind to a halt after they are no longer able to perform it. Where we lack a strong base of leaders we will also find points of weakness and lack of depth to the work.

King was also a visionary who had a brilliant team around him, including the openly gay pacifist Bayard Rustin who helped school him in nonviolent civil disobedience. Rustin was the lead strategist behind the 1963 March on Washington for Jobs and Freedom, but being openly gay impacted public perception and treatment by activists and opponents to the movement. Recognition of his contributions to the civil rights movement has largely come later than it should have, and his story is not situated prominently within the Black radical tradition as it should be. His is not a household name, but it should be. Learning his story helps us to understand the US pacifist movement's relationship to Black liberation work. It also helps us debunk the myth that Black LGBTQ people were not at the forefront of the civil rights movement. There must have been more. Who else have we missed, especially among the young people and the women?

HEALING JUSTICE

There's a running joke among people who know me that I'm not a fan of poetry, and poetry seems difficult to avoid in movement spaces. Often public oration by a poet helps set the tone at a protest or rally. But it was a poet's telling of her encounters with violence and trauma in Palestine, eastern Congo, and Rwanda that gave me the words to understand why I nearly went politically mute after a year of repeated traumatic experiences. Alice Walker's "Overcoming Speechlessness" resonated with me because I, too, witnessed the apartheid project in Palestine and because I could not speak about it with rigor or much depth. I was speechless and unable to explain what I felt and saw after entering the Ibrahimi Mosque in Hebron. I wept after learning of the massacre of twenty-nine Muslims and the injury of more than one hundred during the holy month of Ramadan. I wrote an article that scratched the surface and made Facebook posts and tweets. But due to the heaviness of having seen and experienced pain, I have shared little of what I have witnessed. Armed soldiers in the West Bank. Police officers readying themselves to tear-gas protesters in Charlotte, North Carolina. A young Black person lying on the ground after being shot just around the corner from my home. I've felt heaviness after learning of yet another report of sexual violence within the movement. After visiting incarcerated men in state penitentiaries. After discussing current events with political prisoner Mumia Abu-Jamal. These are things that I have witnessed and encountered firsthand, and I don't speak often of them and of the heaviness and pain they entail. Audre Lorde and Zora Neale Hurston both urge us to speak of pain, to speak of what ails our people. But speaking fully is at times impossible. A feeling of vulnerability stops me. And there is a wall between speaking and speechlessness. I often feel like I am stuck in the wall—in perpetual limbo.

I returned to work after each of these experiences. But processing what I have experienced and witnessed in the span of a year is taking me years to do. I was a full person before these experiences, carrying childhood trauma, teenage trauma, and young adulthood trauma, as you probably do too. So many of us carry the weight of violence and pain. My own trauma shows up when I'm irritable, disruptive, make poor decisions, and become physically ill, depressed, or anxious. These manifestations prevent me from doing my best, but they do not prevent me from showing up.

Our movement needs a complete culture shift. It is especially important for leaders dealing with trauma to check in honestly with themselves and those they trust, to decide if they are *able* to lead. Our hurt comes out against others all too often and prevents us from doing what needs to be done. Sometimes activists have to remove themselves or scale back to take care of their physical and mental health. Movements must retrofit for this reality so that we can all show up as our best selves in our work. As feminist scholar and activist bell hooks writes in *Sisters of the Yam*, "We cannot fully create effective movements for social change if individuals struggling for that change are not also self-actualized or working towards that end. When wounded individuals come together in groups to make change our collective struggle is often undermined by all that has not been dealt with emotionally." Admittedly, this is difficult terrain. People throughout the African diaspora carry centuries of violence from colonialism, slavery, patriarchy, segregation, and economic injustice. Going back to Beth Richie's "violence matrix," the levels of violence we face daily within our homes, communities, and society are off the charts. And there is no wall to keep this dynamic outside of our movement. If there were walls keeping out wounded people, there would be no people to do the work.

Melissa Harris-Perry set the internet on fire in July 2017 when she declared her opposition to self-care. In her piece "How #SquadCare Saved My Life," she refused to "accept that self-care is necessary for health and well-being" and instead argued that only through care from people with whom she is in a deep relationship can she be made well.[1] This presented a dilemma for many activists. On one hand, we are taught and encouraged to sacrifice to no end. Our ancestors and living comrades have made sacrifices beyond what most of us today have made. Who are we to not give our lives to the movement? On the other hand, we are human. We get physically sick, and our mental health can deteriorate with the fast pace and constant demands of the work. So how can we proceed under weight of the multiple systems of oppression? Our movement should live with the tension between self-care and community care. Individual activists should commit to self-care on whatever level they are able to, and communities should commit to creating a culture of care. It does not have to be, and should not be, one or the other.

People who have suffered through traumas, which may or may not be known, are not simply present in our movement. They lead our organizations, take care of our children, develop strategy, and train us on how to become better activists and organizers. Like me, you may be one of these people. I've been expected to live devoid of feelings and to act with grace at all times. And maybe I once held myself to that standard too. Because of this, I've had to fight to cultivate and protect my wellness. I have a robust community of family, friends, generative somatic practitioners, and spiritual models who help me do the self-work necessary to be the human I'm committed to being. And it is a daily struggle that I wasn't trained to engage in by the people who taught me how to be an effective community organizer. I've learned that sometimes self-preservation means not working to solve problems that are not mine to solve. It means taking time to sleep. (I am a chronic insomniac—sleep has been difficult for me for over ten years of my adult life.) Intensive self-work taught me to tend to my own garden so that I may be a better steward in movement work. Perhaps you can relate?

We have a responsibility to do better for our people and ourselves. Many of the movement's newest activists—of any given age, not just young people—have entered movement work during times of crisis and rapid response. Ash-Lee Henderson, codirector of the Highlander Research and Education Center, says, "We don't teach, share, and learn with [new activists] how to move from rapid response into long-term organizing or having long-term strategies." But she notes that people need to know more than simply showing up. "If all I know how to do is turn up, then what I'll do is turn up in the streets against a target, I'll turn up against you, I'll turn up against my partner, I'll turn up because that's all I know how to do, right? . . . [Simply showing up] eventually will wear people down because that's not moving from a place of joy, it's moving from a place of our trauma and crisis."

Movement building is messy and trying and tests every facet of who we are as individuals. It is also beautiful. We are asked (and expected) to give our time, energy, and money. We are expected to share personal stories and to explore what brings us to this work. Giving of ourselves is a constant. Black organizers are often celebrated for superhuman character and mental strength despite living through the daily traumas of being Black and any number of intersecting identities. So many of us have been on the front line of violence from our own people and from the state. Confronting tanks, the National Guard, tear gas, beatings, and jail time takes a high toll on the mental and physical health of activists. So does attending funeral after funeral after deaths of community members. So does sexual violence from strangers or people we've known all our lives. Black people have experienced trauma on many levels, and few of us have the tools to allow us to heal.

While discomfort is a given when we enter many group settings, our movements should not be spaces where the same systemic harms we work to transform are allowed to persist. The movement should allow and create spaces for healing, with the recognition that we cannot do it all. People are affected by factors that have little to do with campaigns, initiatives, programs, and projects. To address this, our movements must prioritize healing justice. According to Cara Page and the Kindred Healing Justice Collective, "Healing justice . . . identifies how we can holistically respond to and intervene on generational trauma and violence, and to bring collective practices that can impact and transform the consequences of oppression on our bodies, hearts and minds."[2] Our movement must invest time and money in healers at least as much as we invest in field organizing. By healers I mean not only those who work in medicine but also those in generative somatics, psychotherapies, and religious and spiritual fields.

"Healing justice is active intervention in which we transform the lived experience of Blackness in our world," stresses Prentis Hemphill, the former director of healing justice at the Black Lives Matter Global Network.[3] Healing justice takes complex work and real commitment, but without it our organizations and people break down.

Movement organizations and individual leaders cannot hold all our trauma. Leaders who know that they are breaking or already broken often fail to remove themselves and instead take out their hurt on everyone around them. Our hurt comes out against each other all too often. But individuals tasked with the work of accountability and healing are too often crushed under the weight, whether intentionally harmful or not, of other people's actions. People are seldom encouraged to remove themselves or scale back to take care of their physical and mental health.

Our communities include far more than people who self-identify as activists, and healers are an important component, especially those committed to healing justice. Some are invested in politics and involved in political strategizing, while others have no interest in that. Healers can be organizers, activists, and strategists—our movement has room for all—and, like any craft, healing work takes study, practice, and resources. The growing number of health-care practitioners in movement spaces and doing healing justice work is promising, although the latter work is sometimes met with distrust and skepticism since it is still new to most people. Healers too require strong support, and healers themselves are sometimes in need of healing.

Healing justice doesn't exist in a vacuum but takes place alongside work against structural oppression. Activist, poet, and performance artist Leah Lakshmi Piepzna-Samarasinha explains that the healing justice movement was born out of a need to respond to "burnout, ableist movement cultures that denigrate and dismiss healing as not serious, a lack of access to high-quality healing and health care by oppressed people." Also proactive, the healing justice movement works to reclaim "the ways our oppressed, surviving communities have always healed, from before colonization to now."[4] Healing justice work is preventive and responsive. It asks us to bring collective practices for healing and transformation into our work.

This is long-term work. It is deep spirit work. How we tap into spirit varies from person to person. I feel it most in large gatherings of our people. I felt it during the Charlotte uprising as I spoke in front of the local police station. I was in the middle of a sea of people, and something came over me. It was an out-of-body experience. I felt that something or someone else spoke through my mouth about the need to abolish policing and prisons. I shouted, "Who keeps us safe? We keep us safe!" This transformed into a call and response so loud that the only sounds I could hear were those of righteous indignation over the violence of policing.

Serena Sebring, a North Carolina–based community organizer, speaks of the personal transformation she felt the first time she and Southerners on New Ground bailed out a Black mother from a Durham jail. She told me that the bailouts made her a believer, and she was moved "by doing street fund-raising and the power of seeing everyday people saying yes to Black women's freedom." The deep spirit work of our movement is possible. Our duty as a movement is to constantly cultivate opportunities for transformation. We must ask ourselves why our movement isn't a place for more of us to be transformed.

When I think about the primary sites of transformation for Black folks, I think about the Black Christian church and its legacy in the Black liberation struggle. Today the church is not the primary site of movement for many of us. Faith leaders must ask why that is the case for so many Black people. I've listened to Black LGBTQ folks and women speak of why they no longer feel at home or welcomed in the church, and they report generations of sexual, homophobic, and transphobic abuse. Of course, some congregations and faith leaders are doing radical Black liberation work. Trinity United Church of

Christ in Chicago, led by the Reverend Otis Moss and young pastors like the Reverend Neichelle Guidry, are good examples, but there should be many more. Despite the church being a site of where transformation is possible, people spend years in various congregations experiencing homophobic, transphobic, and sexist abuse and violence before leaving.

My observation is that people experience such abuse in the movement. Our leaders must also ask why more Black folks cannot be transformed in our movement. It took our ancestors three centuries to overthrow slavery in the Americas. Our vision must extend many generations ahead of us. The ability to plan may feel like a privilege, but we must see it as an imperative. Our ancestors relied on many sources for inspiration and power, including faith-based institutions (e.g., churches and mosques) and others with cultural communities— where people connected to spirit and/or entities beyond ourselves.

What practices can we build for ourselves and our movement to prevent our pain from becoming suffering for the sake of transformation? I took this question, posed by a student during a class I visited at Williams College in 2017, as a challenge and an opportunity to clarify principles behind our struggle.

COMBATING LIBERALISM THROUGH PRINCIPLED STRUGGLE

It is crucial that principled struggle become a cornerstone in the Black liberation movement. It cannot be limited to paid staff members or leaders—principled struggle is imperative for all. Struggle without principles to practice and uphold leads to breakdowns and conflict— and, in some cases, death. Drama is high and on full display in the age of social media. We don't have to talk with ten people to find out about ten different conflicts. We can simply log into Facebook or Twitter and are guaranteed to see posts about conflicts between activists, about grudges or alliances. And since we are committed to improving our lives and those of all Black people, then we need to understand that rumors and unchecked conflicts detract from our ability to carry out effective strategies.

Through principled struggle we can also address the impact of one of the greatest threats to movement building—liberalism. At face value, liberalism is a general philosophy in which liberty and equality are inherent. Sounds great, right? Unfortunately, liberalism requires no specific commitment to collective work, justice, or transformation. It's a breeding ground for indirect approaches and politics that are identity-neutral (unless you're a cisgender white man). Liberalism requires no ideological struggle, and it means, if anything, moderate change so not to ruffle the feathers of too many. I've learned over years that there is no struggle without discomfort. My critique of liberalism isn't about good or bad people. One can appear to treat individuals nicely while supporting policy that kills them. Liberalism dominates discourse about progress in the United States, and our movement must combat it and advance radical agendas for the sake of our collective liberation.

Black radicals have long drawn on the political thought of Mao Tse-tung.[5] During the Black Power movement era, members of the Black Panther Party in Harlem, New York, could be seen on the sidewalks selling *Quotations from Chairman Mao Tse-Tung*, also known as the "Little Red Book," to raise funds.[6] In 1937, Mao laid out why we must combat liberalism. Our movement can no longer afford

> to let things slide for the sake of peace and friendship when a person has clearly gone wrong, and refrain from principled argument because he is an old acquaintance, a fellow townsman, a schoolmate, a close friend, a loved one, an old colleague or old subordinate. Or to touch on the matter lightly instead of going into it thoroughly, so as to keep on good terms. The result is that both the organization and the individual are harmed. This is one type of liberalism.

To indulge in irresponsible criticism in private instead of actively putting forward one's suggestions to the organization. To say nothing to people to their faces but to gossip behind their backs, or to say nothing at a meeting but to gossip afterwards. To show no regard at all for the principles of collective life but to follow one's own inclination. This is a second type.

To let things drift if they do not affect one personally; to say as little as possible while knowing perfectly well what is wrong, to be worldly wise and play safe and seek only to avoid blame. This is a third type.[7]

This stuff kills our movements. The silences around things we know are wrong, like presidents of historically Black colleges and universities meeting with the fascist and white supremacist US president in the White House and organizations accepting funding on behalf of issues and communities they don't actually reflect, work with, or represent. The culture of liberalism in the US social justice movement allows initiatives labeled "progressive" to do harm without consequence. Liberalism entails philanthropic foundations giving millions of dollars to organizations with unprincipled leaders and practices. When these dollars are distributed (in most cases public foundations are bound by law to give), they often involve unnecessary bureaucracy and restrictions in the interests of wealthy funders. Liberalism allows multimillion-dollar budget nonprofits to siphon off the ideas and expertise of grassroots leaders without compensating them and without accountability to communities these institutions claim to advocate for. It allows leaders and organizations to call themselves "progressive" without making commitments to ensuring reproductive freedom or ending mass incarceration or poverty. Liberalism allows so-called progressive elected officials to fund wars but vote no on immigrant rights. In short, liberalism gives room to bullshit.

I've worked in groups in which silence was more common than direct conversations. Time and time again, groups experience conflict but do not confront it until things get so bad that people leave or the climate becomes unhealthy and unproductive. Radical honesty among community members with shared values can be transformative. Frank conversations can dispel rumors about who's getting what money and from where or who said what to whom.

Honesty isn't the same as the transparency I often hear demanded. Information should be available, but information without context is useless. Our movements need honesty, but we also need—and many of us don't have access to—information with context, and we need to know how to make sense of this when we *do* have it. We live in the age of social media where simply expressing disagreement can lead to a public dragging. Such responses are a by-product of the growing culture of purity, in which everything has to be just so within social justice movements, without allowing for differences of opinion, much less for human fallibility. There are days when I wonder why anyone would want to join our movement after seeing how we treat each other online.

Rumors are plentiful in movement spaces. *He said this. They said that. She said something else. I heard this from a reporter and saw this on Facebook.* Social media platforms have not created today's culture of rumors, but they make it easier for rumors to spread and go unchecked. How many times have you heard such things in conversations but heard little, if any, substantiation or verification? It is easier to simply feel anger and frustration than to delve into issues and sort them out in all their complexity. People will say things on social media that they would not dare say to someone's face. I grew up in a place where face-to-face conversation was the most common form of communication. If someone had something to say about someone else, they would say it directly to the other person. In the age of vague-booking (passive-aggressive Facebook posts) and subtweeting (passive-aggressive tweets that don't name names), expressing differences to a comrade directly is becoming less and less common.

If our movement is rigorous in its commitment to healing justice, including transformative justice processes, then each of us has to reckon with how the carceral state has colonized our ways of dealing with conflict. Disposing of someone is an act of punishment. But, as abolitionist and long-time organizer Mariame Kaba says, "punishment is easy, accountability is hard." Removing someone from an organization (an employee or member) or ending a friendship can be done in a principled way. For example, people can be asked to leave because they have a pattern of violating shared agreements, which indicates that they are not willing to change such behavior. Responsibility and action to address the harm are key. It is disposal to blacklist people who *are* willing to take responsibility for their actions or to prevent one from being employed ever again or block one from being in any movement space. But I'm not of the camp that believes that everyone has a place in movement work, even after one has been abusive and violent and caused harm. Some people have to go.

Acceptance of responsibility and the work (as possible) to repair harm to individuals and community: these two things are essential in determining whether someone ought to stay or be required to leave. Asking or demanding that someone leave is not inherently disposal. Asking or demanding that someone leave without due process, study of the situation, and an opportunity to repair the harm: that *is* disposal. In the age of social media, the latter happens more often than the former. People are tried in the court of social media before the family and community they belong to are able to call them and their actions into question. That's unprincipled, and it does not contribute to the project of liberation.

Far too many of us seem to lack the curiosity to ask questions before making conclusions—even when someone in the movement reports abuse or harm from another comrade. I have been guilty of this myself. To my great regret, I've been unprincipled in movement work and had to learn the hard way to investigate before taking action. In this way I once disrupted a meeting in Chicago, thus derailing good work that might have been done. Ultimately, I was agitated to take responsibility for my actions and began to change how I showed up in organizing spaces outside of BYP100.

Rumors and unchecked conflict are security risks. People have died because of these. In 1969, Black Panther Party members Bunchy Carter and John Huggins were killed on the campus of the University of California, Los Angeles, after the FBI spread rumors about them. According to FBI records unsealed years later, the FBI sent the Black Panther Party and the US Organization similar anonymous letters, each saying that a leader of the other organization had a contract out to kill one of its leaders. The resultant rumors and conflict, stoked by the FBI's counterintelligence program (COINTELPRO) led to a physical confrontation that left Carter and Huggins dead. If the tactics sound familiar, it may be because they are echoed by the counterrevolutionary rumor-mongering that happens today via text message, DM, email, and *BuzzFeed* hit pieces. I fear for my own life and the lives of my comrades. I am afraid that I—or someone I work with—will end up dead because of conflicts that could have been resolved without violence.

People do not always act with good intentions or with the community's interests in mind, but we must ask questions and investigate before believing anything that sounds out of place. Dealing with conflict in isolation allows for so many things to go wrong. I've spent months, maybe even years, believing something about someone without taking the time to investigate and corroborate. Investigation can entail asking questions of other people in your orbit or affected by the problem at hand. Investigation can also mean speaking directly with the person said to be causing a problem. While I don't always get it right, I've learned to ask and clarify before I speak with certainty about matters. Principled struggle means that we talk with each other from a place that allows mutual dignity. Principled struggle means that our conclusions about people, events, and organizations are as sound as possible, grounded in observation, and recognizing that even then our assessment may not be valid.

MOVING FORWARD

Our movement is a place where we are often asked to practice and do things that aren't practiced in the broader society. Activists, especially leaders, are expected to be better than everyone else. But movement building requires integrity, not perfection, and integrity means that we own our action and inaction. Committing to integrity instead of perfection leads to real accountability, honesty, and transformation. Integrity is possible when we have many strong leaders and a culture of healing justice, and when we combat liberalism.

Members of the ruling class—including politicians, corporate executives, and families that have been wealthy for generations—get anxious when the masses become conscious and build movements. They worry about the possibility of revolution, about losing power and meeting the same fate to which they've consigned the rest of us. In this elite, a small number of public figures often have the opportunity to represent the many and offer superficial concessions. Democrats consistently play this game with Republicans, regardless of which party is in the majority in Congress. In 2018, leading Democrats in Congress, state legislatures, and city councils are in a state of identity crisis. Their lack of clarity and commitment means anemic—some might say piss-poor—policy affecting the people who voted them into office. Democrats are confused, and their reliance on what they *think* they know isn't working. Many people correctly assess that conservatives act out of fear, but liberals are fearful too.

White rage in the faces of young college-aged people wearing polo shirts and khakis makes liberals fearful. They are fearful because the country they thought they knew is not only slipping away; they realize that it never truly existed.

Let us not get caught in that trap of fear, confusion, or arrested development. We need a powerful revolution of hearts and minds. We can't afford to navel-gaze while media "experts" pontificate on who is or is not truly an "American." Black people have never fit into the mold; we've always forced it into question. Blackness—just as humanity itself—is too big and full of variety for one mold, and that's what makes it fertile ground for revolutionary thought and action.

To build truly emancipatory movements, we must focus seriously on leadership development, healing justice, and combating liberalism. By committing to these three core practices and by acting on them, movements can cultivate radical and even revolutionary means for liberation. Radical means "grasping at the root," and radical demands require work that transforms power relations. Revolutionary work can transform hearts, minds, and worldviews—and thus even systems en masse.

Let us form collective agreements and value integrity over perfection. Let us choose investigation instead of assumption. Let us eschew punishment and hyper-individualism in favor of self-work and healing justice.

CHAPTER 5

FIVE QUESTIONS

I once bristled at the public assertion that today's movement is not "your grandparents' civil rights movement." This, I felt, was disrespectful to the people who came before us. But as I reflected more deeply, I found truth in that statement. This *isn't* the civil rights movement, and that's okay. The institutions that led thought and action then are not the movement leaders now. "The Big Four"—the NAACP, Urban League, Student Nonviolent Coordinating Committee (SNCC), and the Southern Christian Leadership Conference (SCLC)—either no longer exist or hold much less power and influence in Black activism. Today's movement doesn't look or talk or otherwise communicate the same way as those who came before us.

Today's movement isn't the Black Power movement either. The nostalgia of some for the Black Panther Party for Self-Defense, the Black Liberation Army, and the Philadelphia-based group MOVE often overlooks the sacrifices people were forced to make in those organizations and the global context in which they worked. Capitalism was cementing itself as a global practice, while mass incarceration was beginning to take a firm grip on our communities. The crack epidemic hadn't yet hit, and HIV and AIDS were just beginning to ravage our communities. The United States had fought wars against fascist regimes and was enmeshed in a cold war with the communist Eastern Bloc. J. Edgar Hoover's COINTELPRO was killing people, breaking down infrastructure, and curtailing Black Power movement momentum.

Today's movement operates under unprecedented levels of surveillance, but activists and organizers can share information at a speed not possible in the past. Our leaders, during times of heightened activities, are on mainstream news shows. Many Black women, queer, and trans leaders, such as Alicia Garza, Cole B. Cole, and Rashad Robinson, are highly visible and have access to resources to rebuild movement infrastructure. But our visibility is not enough. We still have economic, political, and social interventions to make in organizing our communities.

No one person or single group has ever won something truly meaningful for our people alone. Even Harriet "Moses" Tubman, a disabled abolitionist and the first woman to lead a military raid during the US Civil War, had allies and coconspirators. Tubman helped liberate over three hundred enslaved Africans as an Underground Railroad conductor by working as part of a network of relationships. In first reading about her I learned that she carried a pistol and took no shit, but I read little about the support systems she had as a woman who had narcolepsy and was prone to fall asleep in any circumstance. These "sleeping spells" followed an event that happened when she was about fifteen years old: a two-pound weight, aimed at another enslaved person, hit her head. As a child, I never wondered exactly how Tubman accomplished what she did. Now I understand that she used extraordinary organizing skills but also had assistance to do her work without being killed or losing a single person along the way.

Like the abolitionists of Tubman's time, community organizers today imagine, plan, and act to create change once thought impossible. I know transformative change is possible, even under the worst conditions, because of the actions of the named and unnamed people who began this work long before any of us entered this world. Organized people have changed laws and societal norms in ways that have enabled human dignity for all. In spite of the harsh realities we face locally and globally, some people still have the nerve to believe that something better is possible.

Transformative change is possible through social movements, and these movements are made up of diverse individuals who show up as activists and organizers. Activism is probably the most accessible and common entry point for individuals joining movements. We can all be activists—people who take action on behalf of things we care about. Activists attend rallies, make phone calls, write letters, and speak out against injustice. But not all activists are community organizers.

What does community organizing entail? I believe that two essential elements of it are developing leaders and strategizing to take action. The model of community organizing that I learned and practice is rooted in relationships between individuals working toward the same goal, often with various tactics. Organizers can work within cultural spaces, within issue-focused campaigns, and many other places. I believe in community organizing that works to dismantle systems of oppression and replace them with systems designed to allow collective dignity and power. On different levels we can all do the work of organizing within our communities.

Community organizing is not automatically radical or liberating, and no one person or group has a monopoly on it. Some people organize to *restrict* access to human dignity for others, to dominate and oppress others. Like us, they organize around ideas and require resources. In the run-up to the 2016 U.S. presidential election, young white supremacists organized by weaving a story of oppression fraught with lies. Today's network of white supremacist and nationalist organizations is highly decentralized. Yet these activists are finding ways to construct a tighter and more coordinated movement, aided by the technological developments in communications. While their analysis is based in anti-Black racism, patriarchy, and xenophobia, they believe it enough to organize people and resources around a vision of the world where white men rule. And they co-opt the language and tactics of the same social movements they oppose. Community organizers committed to collective liberation cannot afford to rest on their laurels or be content in feeling morally superior.

Community organizing for our collective liberation requires interpersonal and sound relationships with the natural world around us. I believe in organizing with groups of people to create the type of world we want future generations to live in. The gap between the world as it is and as I want it to be expands and contracts, and I can't control the size of the disconnection, but I believe the gap gets smaller when I organize with people along lines of shared interests, values, and vision.

In Obama's Organizing for America era, community organizing became a buzzword and "organizer" became an identity for anyone who worked on a campaign or talked with people about social justice. Everyone was an organizer. New shops like the New Organizing Institute (NOI) popped up in Washington, DC, where Obama staffers cranked out digital organizing and narrative or storytelling-based strategy training for thousands of people across the country. They recruited people like me to lead training sessions at weeklong boot camps with no pay. I got a lot of great practice and made many connections with activists and organizers. At the same time, the imperfections of white-led progressive institutions became evident, and the NOI folded in 2015 due to internal conflict and funding problems. It wasn't all bad—a lot of Black and Brown folks were employed for a time—but the loss of that space has greatly narrowed the pipeline for people living outside of Washington DC and New York City to access skill-building and job opportunities. I use the New Organizing Institute as an example because it represents what can happen when organizing is taught within liberal frameworks and without clear ideological values and grounding in radical social movement history.

The NOI was not alone in using the boot-camp style of training organizers and paid staff for progressive organizations and campaigns. Older schools that taught community organizing, like Wellstone Action and the Midwest Academy, had to adjust and evolve to meet the growing demand for training relevant to Black and Brown organizers. At that time, around 2009–10, I knew of no Black-led organizing institutes in the country that were grounded in radical politics. I had no political home. I only knew of the NAACP and Congressional Black Caucus as places where one could learn organizing from Black people at the national level. The NAACP didn't feel like home for me, and the Black Caucus was for elected officials. Most of the spaces for explicitly radical Black-led work had few resources or were no longer in existence. I later learned about the Malcolm X Grassroots Movement, SisterSong, and Ruckus Society. Those organizations, and the larger radical movements they operated in, were not prominent in the circles I moved in while living in Washington. Although I tended to be left of the status quo in progressive spaces, I had so much more to learn. Once I moved from the DC area, I was exposed to a whole world outside of anyone who identified politically as progressive and liberal.

My training in northern Virginia taught me the basics of relationship-based organizing. Nearly ten years later, I am clear that some things should be constant. First, any community organizing must address issues of power, relationships, people (the conditions we live in), and change. A discussion about community organizing that fails to address and understand power dynamics is like a big family gathering with no food. Who would want that? Not me. Yes, there are some things that can change with the stroke of a pen, but people and their relationships are—and must be—at the core of long-term transformative change.

There are valuable lessons to be learned from various schools of community organizing, but there is no one correct way, certainly not mine. Centuries of Black resistance show that material conditions of our people improve thanks to the will of everyday people to take collective action on such a scale that it shocks the system. This action has included armed resistance, and it has included nonviolent civil disobedience. The tactics have varied. Everyone invested in collective liberation must answer the following questions critical to determining the health and success of our movements: Who am I? Who are my people? What do we want? What are we building? Are we ready to win?

WHO AM I?

If an activist or organizer tells you that she doesn't do this work for herself, move away as quickly as you can. We all have something at stake. Whether it is caring about the quality of air and water or dismantling prisons, humans always have something at stake individually. And figuring out what that is for you starts with knowing who you are as an individual, what you care about, and why that self-knowledge is necessary for anyone committed to collective liberation. When we bring ourselves into the work, we are not robots: we come as people with histories, experience, knowledge, skills, desires, and traumas. And we all have generations of people at our back who help us make sense of who we are and the work we're called to do.

Given all that our people have been through, there can be no hierarchy of stories among Black people. We come from people who lived under the heels of colonialism and slavery, under domestic and foreign terrorism, and our stories are weapons. They should be used against the lies told about our history, not against our own people. Black folks' stories are diverse and sometimes contradictory, but, as with leaders, our movement is stronger when we value this diversity.

Unfortunately our movement doesn't do well at this. The "oppression Olympics"—arguments over who has had it the hardest—is a constant competition. People compete over what types of stories deserve priority because far too many are marginalized and not heard widely enough. I believe that our movements are stronger when we push ourselves to seek and draw out these stories and center them (and those who tell them). It's in these stories that we are better able to identify multiple streams of repression, resilience, and resistance. For example, imagine if more of the protagonists in stories about mass incarceration were Black women instead of men. That would force activists to develop strategies that address gender, reproductive justice, and parenting in prison. Far too many national campaigns miss this.[1]

Movement building requires people who are clear about who they are and what brings them to their work, but not everyone believes in the significance of their own story. In 2009, I joined a team of people working to train immigrant youth activists preparing for national efforts to pass what was called "comprehensive immigration reform" (CIR), anchored by the Center for Community Change, Reform Immigration for America, and the New Organizing Institute. While the politics of the effort were full of contradictions, the training series brought together many young leaders who would go on to work nationally on immigrant rights and justice. We worked with Marshall Ganz, longtime community organizer and Harvard professor, and his team of trainers, using the public narrative training they had developed. I knew that I loved to train and loved working with young people, and my understanding of immigrant and migrant justice grew through the people I met and the stories I heard. Despite having grown up in a predominately Mexican immigrant neighborhood in Chicago, I had no real understanding of what millions of undocumented people in the United States experience. As a US-born Black person, I knew that access to full citizenship for Black folks was tenuous at best, and that while citizenship would offer security to people, it would not liberate them.

This CIR training had very little participation by Black immigrants, although one session in Florida boasted the most diversity, given the local efforts to build more reflective bases of immigrant activists. During the "story of self" exercise, meant to coax out a compelling three-minute personal story, I met a young Black activist, Marc Simms, who was figuring out his place in the work. We were in groups, and I was likely making rounds to check in on participants when Marc said that he didn't have a story to share. While he was from an immigrant family, my understanding was that he did not connect to the primary issue of immigration reform and dominant stories he'd heard. I challenged Marc, telling him that as a Black person in the United States he automatically had a story. He was receptive, and together we worked through the curriculum, which asked us all to identify a challenge, choice, and outcome in our lives that had brought us to activism. It was there that we would be able to connect with other people who shared our values and vision for the world. That is the crux of grassroots organizing. Our stories are mediums for us to understand ourselves and to understand other people.

I have already related a little of my own story in the preface, but I want to share that it took years and deep reflection to coax out my story. I am the daughter of two parents whose parents migrated from the South. The accent my maternal grandmother carried with her from Greenville, Mississippi, is still in my throat. I first learned how to navigate the world while growing up as a little Black girl in the South Side neighborhood of the Back of the Yards. I recall many nights lying awake listening to trains pass through the industrialized area known for its history of community organizing. Most of the families who lived in the neighborhood during organizer Saul Alinsky's era in the 1930s had moved on to more affluent neighborhoods or suburbs long before my family moved into a small brick house there in the late 1980s.

Like many working parents, mine chose the neighborhood because they could afford it. I understood then, even without the language I have today, that the world we lived in had the power to compromise our dignity and overall wellness. As a child I witnessed and experienced adverse effects of an economy based on extracting this planet's resources and exploiting its people instead of committing to regeneration. My early experiences with power—in my home, the welfare office, and my neighborhood—shaped how I move in the world today.

My angst as a Black girl, Black woman, and later a queer or lesbian-identified college graduate and community organizer has affected much of the work I do today. I wish I could bottle and discard that angst, but it's a constant companion and shows itself daily as I am reminded of why I am rightfully angry about so many things.

I'm angry that I have to jump through hoops to get pregnant as a woman who no longer has sex with men and loves a woman who does not have sperm to give. I'm angry that my mother has consistently had to work low-wage jobs despite her superior skills in caring for other people. I'm angry that the police occupy my neighborhood and that they are more present than quality jobs and services for the people who live in it. I am angry that I cannot control whether someone chooses to rape me. I'm angry that people are caged in prisons and jails. I'm angry that white people seemingly fail to think twice before occupying neighborhoods and spaces with arrogance and lack of connection to the people who are systemically pushed out. I'm angry that our people are still not free. I'm still angry that slavery existed and persists in various forms to this day. I hold a lot of angst and anger—and they both drive my activism and organizing work.

There are few places in US politics for people like me. I am a leftist and I am not white or a man. This is difficult for some people to grasp. I don't fit the archetype of the white union guy or the white dude environmentalist or the white hard-line communist or the white data dude who crunches numbers for the Democratic Party by day and joins the resistance by night. I am a Black lesbian leftist. I believe that capitalism should be dismantled in favor of an economy that is people- and planet-centered. In a world with excess food, no one should go hungry—yet people do. I believe that Democratic and Republican Party politics impede this. I say this all in reiterating that I come to my work with personal history, experience, knowledge, skills, desires, and trauma. Knowing who you are, what you care about, and why: these are necessary for anyone committed to collective liberation.

WHO ARE MY PEOPLE?

Dr. Barbara Ransby, the scholar and community organizer who wrote the most comprehensive biography of Ella Baker, exposed many to Baker's work and legacy. Ransby illuminates why Baker often asked "who are your people?" The answers to this question provide insight and direction for the work each of us can do. "Who are your people?" is a question meant to agitate. It is meant to help us become clear about who we identify with and push us to make connections where they aren't obvious or comfortable. Baker, Ransby writes, "pushed educated college students to see illiterate sharecroppers as 'their people,' their allies and their political mentors. She pushed Northerners to embrace Southerners in principled solidarity."[2] Moving back home to Chicago after living in central Illinois, St. Louis, Washington, and New York City gave me different answers to Ella Baker's question.

I left Chicago at eighteen, traveled about two and a half hours away for college, and rarely came back over those four years. I didn't feel compelled to. I avoided what I would find at home—unstable housing and no prospects for employment—and spent every summer in Bloomington, Illinois. At times I worked two jobs over the summer to make rent and have something left for the school year. My college peers became my people. Chicago and its people, even my own family in some ways, didn't become mine again until I returned almost ten years later. In a note to comrades, friends, and chosen family I'd made over the years, I reflected on this with hopes for more meaningful movement work on the other side of a major relocation.

I told my friends that I was proud of Chicago and its history but not proud of where it seemed to be going. Far too many of our people were struggling, too many public goods and institutions were becoming privatized, and our children were being brutally gunned down in the streets. That's just not acceptable. So I'd decided to go back home to do the work. I transitioned from my role at Color of Change to join Chicago-based National People's Action. It was bittersweet to leave the East Coast that had developed me from young activist to organizer and writer. I was ready to build, both professionally and personally, in the place that had raised me.

Finding my people in Chicago allowed me not only to find home but also to show up as a community organizer in more authentic ways. And there were plenty of people with whom I had to intentionally build relationships. I still enter conversations about "the community," conversations in which I'm taken to be an outsider. I understand much of the sentiment about people who relocate to Chicago (and this can apply to other cities) and assert their own agendas on people who have lived there forever. While I am no longer looking to prove my place in my own community, I understand that the work of building trust never ends.

My people are a North Star for belonging and purpose. I want to believe that I belong wherever there are Black people living in this world, but such a belief is only as good as the work I do to make it real. Black folks are my people, and what impacts one of us affects us all. We all have collective responsibility to take action. I want to aid Black struggles across the diaspora, not just be in solidarity with these struggles. Solidarity all too often means not seeing oneself affected by the oppression of another group. But my aspiration and commitment is to align myself with all Black people and not see my own struggle as worthier or less worthy than any others. I've fallen short of practicing this commitment, and those closest to me have called me to task as a result. In the aftermath of Hurricane Maria's destruction of the US Virgin Islands and Puerto Rico, which exposed a structural disregard for the colonized islands, I had to collect and humble myself, and admit to what I didn't know. The systemic division of Black people throughout the Western Hemisphere is older than the US Constitution. From our families to the diaspora, separation is the work of anti-Blackness. I realized that colonialism had gotten to parts of my mind, too, and that was a hard truth to swallow.

My people are those who can hold me accountable for my actions. I am most immediately accountable to the people with whom I am in a direct relationship. I am accountable to my family, my partner, my neighbors, and the members of an organization I belong to, among others. If I were an elected official, I would be accountable to all of my constituents, not just the people who voted for me. If I were a celebrity artist, I would be accountable to the people who purchased my concert tickets or paid to watch my films. Accountability takes discipline, and relationships matter within our movement. If I claim to act on behalf of any group of people, those people have a say in holding me responsible should I do harm. Our movements must take up the work of real accountability. Calling someone out in isolation does not bring a solution; it takes skilled people within a community to bring about solutions and open pathways. Creating a culture and systems for community accountability, just like community organizing, takes investment in real people and infrastructure.

Our movements cannot afford to treat "the people" as an abstract concept when developing campaigns or building organizations. We have to be specific in order to determine who and what is present or missing. Who do we show up for and who *don't* we show up for when solidarity or coconspirators are called for? Sometimes we are not directly impacted by a specific problem. I am a coconspirator with comrades fighting for immigrant justice, but that's not the struggle for me to lead. That work requires me to be aligned with people and organizations in order to be educated and have my activism on the issue directed. It is easier to support an idea than it is to be in solidarity with specific people. That takes work. One example is how people join calls for solidarity with oppressed groups without names of people or organizations being explicit. Alliance with an idea is not as powerful as real solidarity that shows up and is manifest in action. Solidarity requires more than thinking. It requires action, and it requires us to follow the leadership of those who are the most directly affected.

The anti-Black project of breaking bonds between Black people trafficked to the Western Hemisphere continues today. The assertion that "Black folks don't stick together" endures inside and outside of communities despite example after example of Black people doing exactly that. So many people and institutions in the world teach most people the lie that there are not enough resources to go around. We have been told that we are not human. We have been treated as second-class citizens. The intent of anti-Blackness has always been to divide us to keep us down, so we must fight back not as individuals but en masse—all of us, together. All or none. When we declare with Assata Shakur that we have nothing to lose but our chains, we have to take that seriously. She did not stop at calling for the liberation of some Black people. Her life and sacrifices reflect her vision for all of us. Our struggle is for all of our people. And when you find your people, organize yourselves to create the world where we can all live with dignity.

WHAT DO WE WANT?

The question "reform or revolution?" is often posed in activist spaces, yet I'm not convinced that this is what activists need to ask themselves. Black people in the United States have always required diverse

interventions on a wide scale to make their lives livable and dignified. From Marcus Garvey's mass Black nationalism to lunch counter
sit-ins in the sixties and the rise of a Black feminist movement in the
early seventies, these interventions have been both deeply ideological
and action-oriented. And these interventions often have their roots
in our collective angst. Angst, that "feeling of anxiety, apprehension,
or insecurity," can be debilitating alone, but when harnessed collectively it can lead to the formation and operation of a block club or
something much greater. Recognizing shared angst can unite people
across gang borderlines, across class and gender, even across language
and race. And joining that angst with shared feelings that are more
positive—joy and love, to name two—can be powerful chemistry.
Working to create change, especially transformative change, requires
things of Black people that are both foreign and second nature to us
at the same time.

Working together for transformative change means shared vision,
and it means that there will be moments of discomfort. As an organizer I need to be clear about what I know well but also about what I
do *not* know. I must recognize when I am out of my depth on issues,
ideas, and strategies. Further, the project of anti-Blackness and colonization didn't skip over me. I have internalized ways of being and
understanding just as everyone else in the world has. In my case, I
grew up in a world where blackness was narrowly defined. Gender,
and as a result womanhood and queerness, was even more narrowly
defined. Fortunately I've been pushed and agitated at throughout my
political development, and this has helped me to break out of my
confines. Speaking of which, I learned about the concept of prison
abolition from then-nineteen-year-old Asha Ransby-Sporn during
the convening that led to the founding of BYP100. It was a foreign
concept to me that we could live in a world with no prisons or police.
I had thought of them as inevitable before that. I hope that your
worldview will constantly evolve as mine has.

My years in Washington, DC, and in New York City rooted my understanding of what is possible by way of reform. Reforms are changes that are not structural or do not alter power relations in favor of marginalized and oppressed groups. During that time I was rarely in conversations about what it would mean to completely transform the systems that impact our lives. It was not until I joined the movement community in Chicago that I found myself in spaces where people addressed a need for radical structural change that transforms power relations. Here I found community organizations, scholars, and projects advancing their visions to not only end *mass* incarceration but put an end to the entire system of incarceration. No organization impacted my understanding of this more than BYP100. Building the organization, particularly our work in the Chicago chapter, meant building a vehicle to create the transformative change we believed in. The possibilities I found expressed in Chicago extended my personal vision for what was possible and changed what I wanted in the world.

What kind of world do we want? Our individual and collective visions both matter. Social movements, over time and with much struggle, have achieved various aspects of what they have envisioned, but such achievements have often been tenuous. A new political party in power can jeopardize and even destroy them. Freedoms we once thought were a given are now up for grabs. For example, Black folks continue to organize and fight for full voting rights today. It took the invalidation of one section of the Voting Rights Act by the US Supreme Court in 2013 to strip oversight and accountability for state policies regarding public elections. The wave of restrictive voter ID laws introduced and enacted subsequently, disenfranchising people who have been incarcerated and who are incarcerated, illustrate that no freedom is guaranteed in this country. This isn't limited to voting rights. Access to full reproductive health care and the ability to migrate freely, without criminalization, also depend on who is in political office and on the will of those running advocacy organizations with substantial resources, including labor unions and large nonprofits.

We deserve more than partial freedoms cloaked as pathways to liberation. Freedom is not real if everyone can't exercise it. Liberation entails freedoms, but it is more than that. Liberation is a perpetual project of creating and maintaining right relationships between people and the land we inhabit. And our articulation of how we get there—how we liberate ourselves—matters. As activists, regardless of how much power we hold, what we say we want matters—because in this moment we just might get it. In 2014, BYP100 released the "Agenda to Keep Us Safe," a public policy agenda focused on ending the criminalization of Black people. At the time, people from all sectors of the racial justice movement proposed various reforms to address police violence. Perhaps no other reform has had as much traction as the demand to equip police officers with body cameras. We went back and forth in BYP100 about what position to take on this. Some of our members felt strongly that we should advocate in favor of body cameras. Others felt strongly opposed to this. Today, after several cases in which police officers have been caught killing Black people on camera with impunity (e.g., Walter Scott and Eric Garner), it may seem much easier to make a decision. If I could go back in time, I would have taken a clear stance (as I do today) against supporting the use of body cameras to deter police violence.

In 2014, leaders in our organization and throughout the broader movement had differing levels of trust in the justice system. Context matters. We in BYP100 agreed to advocate for community participation in the decision-making process before taxpayer dollars were spent on body cameras. Instead of struggling with others to advance a more transformative agenda, we compromised. Ultimately this decision was healthier for the organization, but with hindsight I see that we could have gone bigger. We settled on a reformist demand that failed to get at the root of the problem. Regardless of the process of the debate, body cameras would not address criminalization. Police officers can turn cameras off, claim they malfunctioned, or commit acts of violence only to be let off the hook by a judge or jury later. Hindsight is a gift and a source of angst.

The types of demands we make do matter. Demands can be made to the state, corporations, powerful groups, individuals, and even to our own communities. Some demands are our proposed solutions to address problems. Others, such as "Clean Water Now," "Reparations Now," "Books Not Bars!," and "Stop the Cops and Fund Black Futures," articulate the vision we have for the world. The solutions we choose impact the type of change that can happen and the change that actually happens. For example, today's increasingly popular demand to end mass incarceration comes after decades of grassroots activism and community organizing to raise awareness of the prison nation (as Beth E. Richie terms it), the carceral state we live in. One could dissect the demand to end mass incarceration and say that it is reformist because it does not address transforming power and completely dismantling the prison industrial complex. In the vision, people will still be in cages, just fewer than there are now. And this works for the majority of mainstream advocacy efforts because most of us believe that some people deserve to be in prison.

There are millions of people in prison, jail, and walking around with ankle bracelets that monitor and limit their movement. The people who love them are affected by this too. The immense costs of incarceration do not end with building and staffing prisons and jails. Critical Resistance, a longtime organizational leader in the global movement to end the prison industrial complex (PIC), defines the PIC as "the overlapping interests of government and industry that use surveillance, policing, and imprisonment as solutions to economic, social and political problems."[3] The PIC enables people to target other people based on race, gender, citizenship status, ability, and class. The PIC allows individuals and corporations to profit from the punishment of other people. From the media to the manufacturers of prison clothing, people profit from punishment. Our collective vision must include abolition, "with the goal of eliminating imprisonment, policing, and surveillance and creating lasting alternatives to punishment and imprisonment."[4]

Abolition is a demand and vision that rightly identifies the inhumane living conditions people in prison endure and the impact prison has on the families of those incarcerated. It also calls for transformative justice for victims and perpetrators of violence (these groups often overlap). Abolitionists assert that our time, energy, and resources would be better spent on building completely new alternatives instead of improving what has time and again been demonstrated to be ineffective and worse. Viewing the project through a Black queer feminist lens, community organizers can understand this as liberating for all. If we want a world in which conflict and harm are dealt with in ways radically different than they are now, look to Black queer feminism and include the experiences of women, disabled people, LGBTQ people, immigrants, and men who come from a lineage of people in cages. How does prison impact the environment, reproductive justice, and immigrant rights and justice? A Black queer feminist lens focuses on questions like these.

WHAT ARE WE BUILDING?

Each generation of struggle lays the groundwork for the next. In laying that groundwork our movements have consistently encountered many of the same battles. We fight on terrains that we do not control. The deck has been stacked against Black people in this hemisphere since the beginning of the transatlantic slave trade. And still we persist. Our people have built institutions and survived among people and systems set up to kill us. The imperative for today's movement is to not rest on laurels but to instead shift the terrain we fight on. This is fundamentally connected to struggles for power.

What is power? The word has many meanings. Power is the ability to act and get what you want. Power is built and maintained through organized people and organized resources. Power is not inherently good or bad. For people from marginalized groups, experiences with power are often negative. We are used to people having power over us. The amount of power other people and institutions have over our lives, our children, our mobility, our access to basic needs (food, water, and shelter), and even our desire is immeasurable. Lovers, politicians, social workers, teachers, and parents can all wield oppressive power in our lives. Power relationships are based on individuals, but they are intrinsically connected to systems of power maintained by capitalism, patriarchy, white supremacy, and anti-Blackness. A movement for collective liberation must be about changing and transforming those power relationships. This is a tall order.

What type of power do we want? Creating changes requires building and harnessing power. Anyone committed to transformative change must also be committed to building transformative power. What institutions exist today where Black people organize our people and our resources? Who influences the information we receive? Who controls our resources? The answers to these questions go beyond the media and the state and entail more than how the dollar circulates in our communities. Capitalism with "Black" in front of it won't liberate our people. Capitalism is by definition tied to the subjugation of African-descended people. Our collective liberation will not come from models that rely on individual or small group wealth-building. As Audre Lorde teaches, we cannot use the master's tools to dismantle the master's house. Capitalism is highly adaptable, and those who want to maintain it perform any measure needed to save it each time it faces crisis. If we take up the work of prison abolition, the alternatives we have to supply and prepare to build must rely on economic and social models that benefit the greatest number of people, not just a few.

Our work must center self-education and collective education. Intellectual labor and community organizing are essential. The Black radical tradition illustrates that liberation stems from the work of organizations, scholars, and activists, not from one charismatic leader. Study, rigorous discussion, and a lifelong pursuit of knowledge are imperative for each of us. Making education and knowledge accessible to our people requires community organizing too. In a society where most people read at a seventh- or eighth-grade level, our political programs must address literacy and be communicated in various ways, not just in writing. Our people can understand complex ideas, though, and we should not sell ourselves or our communities short. We must work to communicate clearly but also foster our collective ability to articulate and process complex ideas.

Who has power? Today there are far too many allowances for individuals with concentrated power to control what happens in our movements. One example is the power that philanthropic foundations have over resources owed to communities. Funding in today's movement is not based on meritocracy. As in many other sectors, it is based on relationships, visibility, and strategy. After decades of divestment from Black organizing by major foundations, movement groups are now beginning to see resources come their way again, but funding is not a given. Public foundations have money that they must spend for charitable purposes, but application requirements, program officers, and reporting requirements excessively control where and how the money should be spent. Foundations hold too much power over the resources we need to support our movement. At the same time, there are foundations like the Crossroads Fund and the Trans Justice Funding Project that are led by people rooted in the communities they support.

Work needed to change the material conditions of our people is consistently underfunded, and models that have been demonstrated to work remain short of resources. It is easier to write off organizations and people who receive funding from foundations than it is to have a clear understanding of how much it costs to pay for health-care insurance and a living wage in an economy where there is no profit motive to support social change. Community organizers don't have to accept grant money, but in a capitalist economy such work cannot be done without money. People have to feed themselves and their families. Gone are the days when one could work one job and support an entire family.

We need to deeply examine the economic realities of this moment. The civil rights movement was funded by wealthy individuals. The Black Power movement received grants and funding from wealthy people such as Jane Fonda. These movements also had robust revenue-generating models. Are churches a potential source of funding our movement? Selling a newspaper, like the Black Panthers did, is certainly no longer a viable model today. There are models for building resources through socialist frameworks. Membership dues and cooperative enterprises are examples that require skills, time, and infrastructure to implement. Public policy in the United States seems created to prevent our work from being done. Worker cooperatives are illegal in some states. In other states, traditional corporations are rewarded with tax breaks while cooperatively owned companies are not. Community-based solutions are needed, and so are structural changes to our entire economy. Public education should receive more funding than policing and prisons. The *Freedom to Thrive* report, produced by BYP100, Law for Black Lives, and Center for Popular Democracy, found that in Baltimore, for every one dollar the police department receives, public schools receive just fifty-five cents. The report also found that in fiscal year 2017, Chicago allocated almost

40 percent of its $3.7 billion general-fund budget to the police de-partment and 2.1 percent to the Department of Family and Support services, which includes youth mentoring, early childhood educa-tion, violence reduction, summer programs, after-school programs, and homeless services.[5]

As someone who has raised millions of dollars from foundations and individuals, I have always approached fund-raising as a matter of reparations and securing what is rightfully ours. I wrestle with de-veloping strategies that insure that our basic financial needs are met while building alternative resource streams. We need access to land. We need money to pay for the goods and services our families need.

Whether we are building institutions or running experiments, we have to decide what exactly we're doing. If you enter the room expecting to work on a thirty-year strategy while I am expecting to craft short-term experiments, how do we work together? I'm not asking that we find a middle ground—both approaches are neces-sary—but how do we connect those strategies for a larger purpose? Our movement must be flexible enough to deploy multiple tactics and disciplined enough to carry out strategies that move us toward collective liberation.

ARE WE READY TO WIN?

Are we ready to contend for power and create the world we want to live in? Gopal Dayaneni of Movement Generation says that "if we are not ready to govern, then we are not ready to win." He goes further to say that if we aren't ready to govern, then we don't even deserve to win. Governing is not synonymous with becoming part of the governments we live under—or duplicating them. Governing happens whether we like it or not and whether we're involved or not. Governing happens inside and outside of official government in-stitutions. Even within the anarchist movement, with no hierarchy, decisions need to be made. Governing is the process of making decisions that impact groups of people. How are we governing in our organizations and communities? Decision-making in these sites of public government impacts the private decision-making in our families and relationships. Governing impacts every domain of our lives. Our movements must and can work toward a decision-making culture that produces different terrains in which we live our lives.

The time is now to experiment and implement practices that match the type of world we want to create. We don't have to wait until every prison is emptied to deal with conflict and harm without resorting to punishment. Are you working to phase yourself out as a leader so that others can shepherd the work in the next generation? Are you communicating information and sharing resources to increase knowledge and support vital community organizing? How do we deal with violence and people who harm others? We can combat liberalism and provide models to help our people along the way. Sometimes actions happen simply because people are fed up and decide to do something about it. More often than not, once the moment of rapid response passes, people begin to talk about what happens next.

I don't know what democracy looks like outside of the practices and cultures we've built within various movement spaces. Many times it feels like we're playing governance, just like we played house as children. Some people can borrow from and incorporate Indigenous governing practices, but many of us have no clue our ancestors made decisions before colonialism and the transatlantic slave trade. And of what we *do* know, not all of it is what we want today. Patriarchy existed prior to colonialism. We can build from what's come before us and innovate at the same time. The United States is one massive lie and one massive truth. Democracy and the promise of perfecting it in this country is one of the biggest lies ever told. We have never had a true democracy in this country. At best, the system was designed by and works for people who meet the standards of those in power.

One massive truth is that it was designed for white men who were property owners (owners of land and people) and that it works best for white people and those identified in closer proximity to whiteness and those far away from Blackness. It works best for Christians and Jewish people. It works best for citizens who are male, able-bodied, heterosexual, and cisgender. If you don't fit into those boxes then it is likely that your people have had to fight for rights and the power to govern and not just be governed. And this dynamic continues today with an inability to govern in the public space.

Let's change the terrain and conditions of our collective struggle. We can build movements that transform the political and economic terrain. We can also change the terrain of determination, to one of self-determination regarding our desires, our bodies, and the communities we live in. Self-determination is not an individualistic concept. Instead it entails a body of communities—and those who make up communities—determining how they will thrive and how their lives are lived. Right now, the government, corporations, and wealthy individuals hold more power over our lives than many of us do. That must change. Having the ability to build communities centered in people's needs and stewardship of the earth shouldn't be a radical idea. Making collective decisions about how our lives are lived is governance. It's in that space that we can live out the project of collective liberation.

CHAPTER 6

THE CHICAGO MODEL

I was leaving the South
to fling myself into the unknown. . . .
I was taking a part of the South
to transplant in alien soil,
to see if it could grow differently,
if it could drink of new and cool rains,
bend in strange winds,
respond to the warmth of other suns
and, perhaps, to bloom

—RICHARD WRIGHT

We do this for Marissa
We do this for Mike Brown
We do this for Rekia
We do this for Damo,
We do this till we free us.

—KUSH THOMPSON AND MALCOLM LONDON,
BYP100 Chicago

If we drew a map of the creation story of the Black radical tradition, Chicago and its people would appear at nearly every critical point in time. Movement building and victories in Chicago have made national and international news in recent years, but the city has been a vanguard of radical Black activism and culture since the Great Migration. Early in the twentieth century Black migrants were encouraged to come to the city. In 1916, the *Chicago Defender*, one of the nation's most influential newspapers, called Black people North. "If you can freeze to death in the North and be free, why freeze to death in the South and be a slave? *The Defender* says come."[1] And they came in the hundreds of thousands seeking the "warmth of other suns."[2]

Black people leaving the South to escape terrorism and poverty brought knowledge and culture to Northern cities. There they were met with violence from northerner employers, land barons, and the police. There they joined Black people who had long lived in cities from Chicago to Detroit and New York. But Chicago was special. Here migrants from Mississippi laid down new roots, while Black cultural giants like Langston Hughes and activists like Ida B. Wells were also drawn to the city. The Chicago Black Renaissance, while less known than the Harlem Renaissance, holds a place in the making of the Black radical tradition.

Despite new pathways to prosperity, poverty and systemic violence didn't disappear. Black folks were often quarantined to the worst housing in the city. Redlining, a practice of literally drawing lines on the city map to delimit where black people could and could not live, was a different form of apartheid than the one migrants had experienced in the South. The people who controlled Chicago's real estate market perfected this practice. Lorraine Hansberry entered the Black literary canon with her play *A Raisin in the Sun*, in which she told the story of housing segregation through the experiences of the Younger family. In Chicago, cultural work cannot be separated from movement work.

Work on the ground in Chicago is now led in many cases by descendants of people who made the journey north and stayed. We are the grandchildren and great-grandchildren of those who sought out the warmth of other suns, who lived, dreamed, fought, and were sometimes slain inside and outside of the red lines. We drop r's in our speech and fill church pews and mosques. We fight in remembrance of the murdered Emmitt Till and his mother, Mamie. Our parents worked to elect Harold Washington, our city's first Black mayor. We never fully left the South—it still lives within us. The South is in our speech and on our plates. We come from elsewhere too, including Haiti, Nigeria, Ethiopia, and Belize. We are Black Chicagoans, still loving, resisting, creating models, and advancing even in the face of entrenched adversaries. We are not the East or West Coast. We are not the South. Chicago exists squarely in between. We are at the nexus, building a movement unique to our place but also impacting national and global movements for liberation.

We are holding on as the Black population experiences mass displacement and violence from inside and outside our communities. Our work models how to organize in one of the last US outposts for Black culture. Not a week goes by without a story about the gentrification of Harlem or DC crossing one of my social media feeds. While these East Coast meccas receive the most press, it would serve us well to be informed by the history of anti-eviction organizing in Chicago. Communist-inspired organizing in the 1930s is said to have been able to mobilize five thousand people in less than thirty minutes to stop an eviction.[3]

Chicago is full of contradictions. If you meet a Chicagoan, you'll likely know it within fifteen minutes of conversation. We boast about but lament our dear city, and many of us choose to remain here—and will always live here—regardless of the challenges. Chicago, on the one hand, has every amenity a city can offer. On the other hand, high unemployment rates, police and other surveillance, intra-community violence, and chronic mental health problems plague Black communities. Black resistance is in a direct relationship with Black repression. Black movements are so intense because Black communities have been petri dishes for state-sanctioned repression, violence, and apartheid. While Blacks migrants came to Chicago to escape terrorism, they were met with terror—from police, slumlords, and white communities who wanted to keep them out.

Historian Darlene Clark Hine describes Chicago's Black communities as a collection of northern southerners and southern northerners, meaning that migrants held dual experiences.[4] As a result of the community makeup, Black organizing in Chicago draws on traditions and tactics of the South and the North. This means we are able to move slowly and quickly. It means we can hunker down for long-term campaigns and turn up because it's a Tuesday. And, like our city, the movement is windy: situations can change quickly, alliances are not always obvious, and a boundary can be crossed without you even knowing it.

Today Chicago is the site of campaigns that illuminate the impact of policing on Black women, that call for deep investment in our communities, and that demand an end to state-sanctioned violence. Together people and groups of differing political orientations have come together, using various tactics, and won battles—from the Trauma Center Campaign's success, to the hunger strike and organizing that led to keeping Dyett High School open, to the 2016 ousting of Cook County state's attorney Anita Alvarez for a pattern of mishandling cases.

Our calls to #StopTheCops and #FundBlackFutures recognize the heavy impact of poverty, violence, and trauma upon Black Chicagoans. Organizers took to the streets in 2015 when the city hosted the conference of the International Association of Chiefs of Police (IACP), bringing over fourteen thousand police chiefs from across the world to Chicago. BYP100, in collaboration with groups including Assata's Daughters, We Charge Genocide, #Not1More, Organized Communities Against Deportations (OCAD), and Lifted Voices, led a civil disobedience action to shut down the opening events of the conference. The IACP was returning to Chicago—it had hosted its first conference there, in 1893—and its original purpose still held, serving "as a means to apprehend and return criminals who [have] fled agency jurisdictions in which they were wanted."[5] We understood that the IACP was true to its roots in the nineteenth-century patrols formed to capture enslaved Africans seeking freedom, and we intended to send a message to the Chicago Police Department, the IACP, and the broader organizing community.

On October 24, 2015, we locked down four blockades inside and outside of McCormick Place, the site of the police conference. We understood this convention to be a gathering of minds to plot out the continued domination of Black people around the world. Sixty-six of us were arrested that day. It was the biggest investment in direct action and civil disobedience that BYP100 had ever made. The goal, as in any strategic civil disobedience, was not to be arrested for the sake of theater. The goal was to demonstrate how far we were individually willing to go to call out the systemic violence of policing in the world and to demand investments in Black communities (and defunding of police). Despite intensive preparation and the large scale of the action, many people have never heard of it. Our strategy lacked a clear communications plan. Commitments from partners fell through and we failed to have backup plans on the ground. It was a lesson in the need to invest in strategic communications just as much as we did in everything else.

That action gave birth to our "#StopTheCops and #FundBlack Futures" campaign. BYP100 brought in members from our New York and DC chapters, our newly formed Detroit chapter, allied organizations, and trainers from the BlackOut Collective to support the action. In this collaboration we learned and gained capacity to work together, and the efforts of the Black direct action can be seen in organizing to this day.

Getting to the point where we could collaborate on a large-scale action, however, took months of work and relationship building. When BYP100 entered the Chicago organizing community after its founding in 2013, we were met with mixed reactions. Many people supported us and found our group of young Black people refreshing and inspirational. But many of us were queer, transgender or gender-nonconforming, and women—and thus we were also met with distrust. BYP100 members (in Chicago and chapters forming in Washington, DC; New York City; the San Francisco Bay Area; and Philadelphia) made the decision to build a membership-based organization. We chose to use conventional organizing methods including building a membership base and providing skill training. We also chose to use organizing methods rooted in cultural work, investing in young peoples' leadership at every level of the organization and Black feminist ideology in an organization of all genders. We could have made different choices, but we did not—because we believed that our method was a true path to transformation. In doing so, we made interventions that shifted the organizing climate in Chicago (and across the nation), and we learned many lessons from the mistakes we made along the way.

I had moved back to Chicago from New York City about six months before our founding. Very few people knew who I was, and in true Chicago fashion I was met with mostly reasonable skepticism. I remember boarding the shuttle to the BYP100 founding convening and being met with looks that said, "Who is she, and why is she the bus captain?" Had anyone said to me "here's what you need to accomplish by 2015," I would have turned around and walked the other way. I remember leaving Ferguson, Missouri, during the uprising there, earlier than many other comrades—to get back to our very first direct action targeting the Chicago Police Department. It was August 2014. That one action calling for CPD to decriminalize marijuana led to a long-term engagement with the third-largest police force in the United States. CPD's leaders and other city officials would get to know our work well as we led and joined efforts across the city to expose police corruption and the systemic violence perpetrated by the institution. BYP100 joined a collection of groups led by young Black people, including a mixture of born-and-raised Chicagoans, transplants, and native transplants like myself who had grown up in the city yet had never organized there. Some groups had sprung up in the aftermath of the killings of Trayvon Martin and Mike Brown. Others, like Fearless Leading by the Youth (FLY), created years before, aimed to secure justice and community investments after the death of a comrade.

BYP100's work didn't end with our efforts focused on the Chicago Police Department. Our organization joined the Fight for 15 Campaign locally and nationally, and we brought new leaders to work on its international efforts to mandate a living wage across industries that disproportionately employ Black people. We joined forces with organizations including OCAD and Mijente in the struggle to end the criminalization and deportation of immigrants.

This work did not begin with BYP100. There is a long legacy of anti-policing organizing and community building in Chicago. For example, the Chicago Alliance Against Racist and Political Repression (CAARPR) formed in 1973 out of the mass movement to free Angela Davis and all political prisoners. The Black Panther Party Chicago chapter laid groundwork for cross-movement collaboration, and the 1969 assassinations of Chicago Panther leaders Fred Hampton and Mark Clark show that Chicago has long been a site of state repression against our movement.

I was not present in the development of every campaign and effort discussed in this chapter. I am positive that individuals closest to the work will find my accounts insubstantial. My intention, though, is to highlight what I have learned and observed as an organizer and history nerd in order to illustrate unique paths of community organizing in Chicago since the 1970s. I've worked alongside people, young and old, who know this history better than I do—because they were there.

REPARATIONS WON

Between 1972 and 1991, Chicago Police Department commander Jon Burge and police detectives under his command tortured Black people, including women and over one hundred men, in part to elicit confessions. Their tactics included electric shock and suffocation. This abuse and sanctioned torture resulted in forced confessions and long prison sentences and death sentences for people taken into custody in the CPD's Areas 2 and 3, both predominantly Black neighborhoods. There are still men in prison today who were convicted after confessions under torture. I've met at least one torture victim serving a sentence, during a visit to Stateville prison in 2016. I've also met Darryl Cannon, who spent twenty years in prison after a forced confession. CPD detectives subjecting Cannon to torture in 1983 enacted "mock executions by stuffing a shotgun in his mouth, hit him with a rubber hose, and shocked his testicles with a cattle prod." The sadism was "something that they liked doing," says Cannon.[6]

These injustices were met with resistance by the torture victims, their family members, and community members, but the journey for justice has been a long haul and has involved dozens of organizations, legal advocates, artists, and groups such as the Chicago Torture Justice Memorials. The innovative effort spans decades. Through many tactics, the effort focused on holding Burge, the officers under his command, public officials, and the City of Chicago accountable for the physical, mental, and spiritual violence inflicted as elected officials, including the often-celebrated Mayor Richard M. Daley, stood by and did nothing.

Throughout the 1980s, over fifty organizations, including Citizens Alert and the Task Force to Confront Police Violence, led consistent actions outside of City Hall. In 2004, a coalition including ex-gang member and civil rights attorney Standish Willis, decided to tell the story to an international audience. Willis felt that they "could make the torture case international, and embarrass the United States." Indeed the United Nations did call on the US government to investigate.[7] Black people had taken various causes to the United Nations in the past. That tactic can strip the supposed moral superiority of the United States as unfounded, and such international exposure can produce effective results. Winning a reparations campaign was deemed impossible by many, but Willis and Black People Against Police Torture also birthed the idea that Chicago police torture victims should demand reparations.

Today's demand for reparations for descendants of slavery in the United States is a part of a long-standing movement. The National Coalition of Blacks for Reparations in America (N'COBRA) defines reparations as "a process of repairing, healing and restoring a people injured because of their group identity and in violation of their fundamental human rights by governments or corporations. In addition to justice, it is a principle of international human rights."[8] And despite successful reparations efforts for other groups of people systemically targeted by violence, including survivors of the Jewish Holocaust, reparations for descendants of enslaved Africans are consistently marginalized in progressive politics. In defense of their anti-reparations stance, white people often proclaim that *they* didn't own slaves. This position represents not only ignorance of history but also a failure to recognize and accept how they continue to benefit from slavery. The terrorism of Jim Crow in the South, the violence of economic oppression and poverty in the North, the so-called war on drugs, and today's prison industrial complex all support the argument for reparations to address centuries of domination of Black Americans.

The police torture victim reparations campaign addresses both the needs of people injured and the need for systemic changes to improve the material conditions of Black communities in Chicago.

It builds on previous successful campaigns led by torture victims inside and outside of prison. For example, ten police torture victims, who called themselves the Death Row 10, in the first years of the new millennium successfully collaborated with the Campaign to End the Death Penalty and the Illinois Coalition to Abolish the Death Penalty. Their organizing resulted in Illinois governor George Ryan commuting the sentences of all death row inmates and pardoning four of the ten men in 2003.

Organizing for justice in Chicago requires groups of oppressed people to make connections with each other's causes and for those who are directly affected to lead, even if they are in prison. As the police torture victim reparations campaign advanced, many stakeholders and decision-makers joined the effort and reached communities across the city. Joey Mogul, the People's Law Office attorney and co-founder of the Chicago Torture Justice Memorials project, drafted the original reparations ordinance, which served as a basis for a package introduced to Chicago's city council by Aldermen Howard Brookins and Proco Joe Moreno in 2013. The reparations campaign invited newer legal advocates, cultural workers, activists, and community organizers to align themselves with the struggle of police torture victims and their families. Two years later, the campaign was a success. Reparations won included

- a formal apology for the torture by Chicago police during the time the CPD was headed by Jon Burge;
- specialized counseling services to the torture survivors and their family members on the South Side;
- free enrollment in city colleges and job training for survivors and family members (including grandchildren) as well as prioritized access to other City of Chicago programs, including help with housing, transportation, and senior care;

- a history lesson about the torture cases, taught in Chicago public schools to eighth and tenth graders;
- the construction of a permanent public memorial to the survivors; and
- $5.5 million set aside for the torture survivors.[9]

Seemingly overnight, the campaign slogan "Reparations Now!" was transformed and printed on T-shirts proclaiming, "Reparations Won." This was a people's victory. This victory, made possible by the tenacity of the police torture victims and their families, organized people around a single goal while allowing multiple entry points for people of different generations and races and with differing experiences and skills. BYP100 didn't exist when the struggle for torture justice began, nor did newer organizations such as We Charge Genocide, which became an anchor in the campaign. Young people, many of whom were activated by the Ferguson uprising, boosted the momentum of the reparations campaign. We joined efforts to call city council members, led direct actions targeting Mayor Rahm Emanuel, and used social media to raise community awareness. And we won, despite the doubts, which would not have been possible without the work done before many of us became activists and community organizers.

The intentionality to address the needs of individual torture victims and their families was extended to children in Chicago's public schools. The people who crafted the campaign saw that education could help prevent police torture and such atrocities from happening again. The campaign's demand for a community center and mental health support for survivors and their families also points to the structural and long-term changes its organizers sought. Oppressed people and their leaders clearly were looking beyond individual gain, while providing a model for what abolition can look like in actual practice.

The statement released by Amnesty International USA, the Chicago Torture Justice Memorials, Project NIA, and We Charge Genocide describes the significance of this victory beyond the city:

> Chicago is the first municipality in the history of the United States to ever provide reparations for racially motivated law enforcement violence. In doing so, the City of Chicago is agreeing to acknowledge the City's responsibility for gross human rights violations and to commit significant resources to begin to help repair the harms inflicted on the torture survivors, their families and the communities they come from. The enactment of this legislation sends a strong message that activism and organizing matter in the ongoing struggle for human rights and social justice.[10]

To organize successfully in Chicago means being in it for the long haul. It takes creativity, endurance, and a degree of hardiness. (To honor our fallen we do actions no matter the weather, even in the middle of frigid winter.) Our victories don't come easily or quickly, and the campaign to secure justice for survivors of police torture in Chicago is emblematic. The Chicago organizing community manages to do more than one thing at a time. As the campaign for police torture victims was waged and won, campaigns were underway addressing other areas of structural violence throughout the city.

A VANGUARD EMERGES

The escalation in organization of direct action led by young Black people has undoubtedly impacted the broader social justice organizing community in Chicago. It is difficult to mark the beginning of this period of the Black liberation movement, to say just when young Black people began to exert leadership not seen since the Black Power movement. I was introduced to youth-led direct action in Chicago while attending and supporting actions to stop the deportation of undocumented immigrants. I remember the first time I saw a lockbox, which is a piece of equipment used in civil disobedience blockades. It locked together the arms of immigrant leaders who were shutting down Michigan Avenue to disrupt a planned fund-raiser headlined by then president Barack Obama. I was fascinated and remember thinking, *Will I ever do this?*

Around the same time, the Trauma Care Coalition led by young Black leaders in FLY and members of Southside Together Organizing for Power (STOP) held various civil disobedience actions against the University of Chicago to secure its demands to build a comprehensive trauma center on the city's South Side. This fight was rooted in outrage and pain caused by the death of the youth leaders' comrade Damian Turner, who died at eighteen after being rushed from the South Side neighborhood of Woodlawn to Northwestern Medicine's location in downtown Chicago in 2010. They believed that he would still be alive had the University of Chicago, just minutes away, accepted shooting victims like Damian. Nearly five years later, the Trauma Care Coalition won. Because of their efforts the University of Chicago committed to build a Level-1 adult trauma center on the South Side. This victory is another example of what it means to organize for the long haul in Chicago.

That same year many of the same Chicago organizers leading in the aforementioned campaigns shifted the national organizing landscape again. Our efforts served as a catalyst for mass #SayHerName mobilizations to end state-sanctioned violence against Black women and girls. #SayHerName, from a phrase coined in a report coauthored by Andrea Ritchie and Kimberlé Crenshaw, was a campaign that also focused on police violence against gender-nonconforming people. What most people don't know is that the #SayHerName mobilizations were rooted in the story of Rekia Boyd.

Rekia Boyd was a twenty-two-year-old Black woman gunned down by Chicago police officer Dante Servin in 2012. The effort to secure justice in this case began shortly after her death. Rekia's family and community activists including Crista Noel of Women's All Points Bulletin were among the first people to fight for justice. Servin was charged with manslaughter because of their efforts. Chicago police officers who kill people rarely ever see a day in court, but in 2015 Servin went on trial, and community members and Rekia's family showed up en masse. One day during the trial, I sat next to Rekia's mom, Angela Helton, and I recall her saying to me, in a voice heavy with grief, "They never talk about the women and girls." In her grief but showing resilience, she spoke about how the best-known stories of police violence entailed Black men and boys. She planted a seed in me that day, and fortunately our movement was poised to change the dominant story. That night after Servin's case was dismissed, some people gathered to meet and discuss our next steps. Servin was still employed by the CPD, so there was discussion of building a campaign to call for Servin's firing at the next Chicago Police Board hearing, scheduled to take place on May 21, 2015.

Comrades from the Movement for Black Lives, including Mervyn Mercano, Patrisse Cullors, Maurice Mitchell, and Thenjiwe McHarris, reached out to me that week, and they asked how they could help. The idea of calling for a national day of action was proposed. I then went back to BYP100 and other organizations to see what they thought about making the call. There was support, so from there we began to organize a national day of action to take place on May 21. At some point, Andrea Ritchie contacted me and asked if it made sense to release the #SayHerName report on the same day as the police board hearing. That led to connecting the work she and Crenshaw had produced to a grassroots effort already in motion. Together we wove a narrative about the impact of policing Black women, girls, and gender-nonconforming people that changed how everyday people understood the meaning of #BlackLivesMatter. The nexus of Black women's intellectual labor and grassroots organizing led to powerful actions across more than sixteen cities in the United States on the same day. The moment Rekia's mom joined the Chicago action, I looked at her and said, "Ms. Helton, I remember sitting in the courtroom with you that day, and you shared that no one ever talks about Black women and girls. Well, we're changing that all over the country today."

The Fire Dante Servin campaign continued for almost a year from the date of the first #SayHerName National Day of Action. Because of our work and the efforts by Rekia's brother Martinez Sutton and local leaders including Rachel Williams, the national and local narratives of policing began to shift. The campaign showed up at police review board meetings held at CPD headquarters every month for an entire year. The story got bigger, meeting attendance increased, and people began to tell stories that were more and more complete. Collective solutions beyond reform grew clearer for many people. Black women and girls became less of a footnote and more front and center in the dominant understanding of how much is at stake for Black people in the struggle to end policing. The campaign pushed and succeeded at almost every step in securing Servin's termination. Just before the last hearing to determine his fate, Servin resigned. But no campaign could bring Rekia back to life. Our work then was, as it remains, to advance structural changes so that no more families have to go through what Rekia's family continues to cope with today.

SIXTEEN SHOTS AND A COVER-UP

There are campaigns that ignite the hearts of local organizers enough to catalyze unprecedented action, and there are campaigns that capture the hearts of organizers across the nation enough to inform campaign models for victory. The efforts to oust Cook County state's attorney Anita Alvarez, culminating in 2016, is the archetype of both. And Chicago provided fertile organizing ground to make it happen. It took multiple organizations, numerous strategies, various tactics, and a shared goal to get the job done. Groups including Southsiders United for Unity and Liberation (SOUL) and Action Now had begun their efforts to highlight Alvarez's repeated moral and governing failures on issues of criminalization and policing more than two years before she was ousted. BYP100 joined those efforts and later led its own voter engagement program. Electoral campaigns are difficult to gain buy-in for with people who are rightfully distrustful and disillusioned with the voting process. But we did the work because we understood that Alvarez and her office held too much power over our lives and did unconscionable things under the protection of state power.

Like the campaign for reparations, the energy and risk-taking nature of young Black activists breathed energy into ongoing efforts to dismantle the criminal justice system. We Charge Genocide took Chicago police violence to the United Nations and once again turned international attention to the conditions of Black people living in a police state. Their work to highlight the out-of-control spending on policing was crucial in building a larger narrative in calls for justice throughout the city. That work, combined with many other efforts, allowed people to understand how Alvarez, Garry McCarthy (then police superintendent), and Mayor Emanuel could cover up the police killing of seventeen-year-old Laquan McDonald.

William Calloway, a long-time activist, smelled a cover-up and took action. His gut feeling led his joining journalist Brandon Smith in filing a Freedom of Information Act (FOIA) request to release dash-cam footage of the fatal shooting. More than a year passed after Laquan's death—with multiple refusals from CPD and Mayor Emanuel—before a judge ordered the release of the dash-cam footage in November 2015. I, along with other organizers, sat in the courtroom as the judge announced that the CPD and the mayor's office had to make the footage public. I remember feeling somber and grounded yet not sure what would happen next. Our crew left the courtroom, bypassed all of the cameras, and began to assess our next steps.

Just as the court decided to release the footage showing Laquan's execution, the court date for most IACP action arrestees was scheduled. Prior to then most of us had anticipated that we would go to the court adjacent to the police precinct where we had been held after arrest (and where torture had taken place during the CPD's Burge era), and that there we would have our cases dismissed. Instead we launched a new effort after learning that the mayor's office had reached out and requested a meeting with our groups. After much discussion among ourselves, it became clear to us that the mayor's request to meet and discuss the video release was a ploy to control us, not to actually discuss meeting our demands for his resignation and for the city to divest from policing and invest in our communities. So we declined a private meeting with the mayor's office. A group of organizations including BYP100 Chicago, Assata's Daughters, FLY, We Charge Genocide, Black Lives Matter Chicago, and the #LetUsBreathe Collective issued a joint statement that said we held zero confidence that the mayor would be accountable to Black people.

It was clear that the emperor had no clothes. We made a decision to wield our power differently, and the mayor and his administration instead met with other community leaders. Our response shook the administration and some liberal activists. Remembering the night that the video was released and the following events is painful for me. I remain unable to watch the actual footage (enough people saw it, so I didn't have to), but the events that followed the video release are among the most difficult I've experienced in my life. I made some decisions that were strategically smart and others that were out of line with the type of person and leader I aimed to be. And although I am sharing this story years later, it still feels fresh.

Following the judge's decision and after a series of meetings, many of which took place at the STOP office, the group of leaders called for a mass action after the video was released. We decided to establish a space for Black rage and not attempt to police the feelings people held. We marched from the campus of the University of Illinois at Chicago, on the corner of Halsted and Roosevelt. Our first stop was the building where a "community event" organized by Alvarez's office was to be held. SOUL, Action Now, and the Workers Center for Racial Justice had already arrived. Our goal was to disrupt the meeting and ensure that it did not happen. I remember banging against the door alongside FLY leader Veronica Morris Moore, talking with Alvarez's chief of staff, and questioning the young Black man about his love for his people. That night we shut down major streets from Halsted to far into downtown Chicago. Our group grew to hundreds of people by the end of the night.

There was one moment when we stood in a large circle at the intersection of Roosevelt and Wabash, near the CTA train elevated above us. People on the platform listened as we spoke about the killing of Laquan McDonald and called for the resignation of Mayor Emanuel, police superintendent McCarthy, and Cook County state's attorney Alvarez. I will always remember the young Latina who came down from the platform and locked arms with me. She said that she knew about the video and felt that she needed to join us. I am almost certain that this was her first experience of engaging in civil disobedience.

Right as we headed up Michigan Avenue toward the Magnificent Mile and attempted to turn on Lake Shore Drive, a melee with CPD officers ensued. Police threw bikes, pulled hair, and attempted to make arrests. I didn't then know who he was, but I threw myself on top of Vic Mensa to stop his arrest. Comrades pulled each other away from cops and formed a blockade to prevent further assaults from the cops. Three people—Johnae Strong, Page May, and Troy Alim—were arrested. We then headed to the police precinct to call for their release. That night as those three were released, Malcolm London was arrested. As described earlier, a series of painful experiences followed immediately.

Two days later, in the midst of a mass march to disrupt Black Friday shopping, several young Black women and LGBTQ folks were assaulted along the route by individuals who claimed to be aligned with the movement for Black liberation. We were physically and verbally attacked. In the aftermath, BYP100 and many young Black movement leaders, including me, had never been more visible. Reports that BYP100 was funded and controlled by white Jewish men at the University of Chicago were shared on social media. Cathy Cohen and I were targets for homophobic attacks online where individuals cautioned parents to keep their children away from us. I don't share this seeking empathy or accountability but as a caution, to highlight how fissures that may seem minuscule or irrelevant can become deep chasms and prevent work from being done.

As 2016 approached, we barely rested and continued our efforts despite fatigue and growing fears of increased repression (by the state and people who should have been comrades). Chicago and its organizers made the killing of Laquan McDonald a national issue. We called for the resignations of Emanuel and Alvarez and for the firing of McCarthy. While McCarthy ultimately was fired, we still had much more to do.

In early 2016, the campaign to oust Anita Alvarez picked up speed. BYP100 continued its voter engagement efforts through street teams, phone-banking, and political education sessions. Several grassroots organizations continued their electoral campaigns to oust Alvarez and in some cases advocate for her opponent Kim Foxx. One political education session focused on why the state's attorney race was so important to Black communities. We understood that the office held too much power over our lives, so we had a duty to hold Alvarez accountable. A message for young people to simply vote would not be enough. Our work was in communicating why this election mattered.

Then a collective of young Black organizers from FLY, Assata's Daughters, BYP100 Chicago, #LetUsBreathe Collective, Black Lives Matter Chicago, We Charge Genocide, and other groups ratcheted things up a notch and created an arm of resistance and education under the #ByeAnita banner. Longtime scholar, community organizer, and leader Mariame Kaba describes the #ByeAnita campaign "as one arm of a larger electoral organizing effort to defeat Alvarez. But it energized particular populations that do not usually focus on local races and especially prosecutor elections."[11] The campaign, launched in the aftermath of mass protest mobilizations in defense of Laquan McDonald, used direct action, social media, street canvassing, and arts-based tactics to engage young Black people in the electoral process and advance demands to address structural violence in Chicago. That work was done and led by young Black women and femmes from multiple organizations and flanked by members of allied groups who understood the need for their voices to be heard. These leaders reflect years of work, development, dreaming, and experimentation. In March 2016, Chicago's organizing community won: Alvarez lost the election. As Tess Raser of Assata's Daughters said, "Kim Foxx did not win this campaign; Anita Alvarez lost this campaign because we pushed this city to see what Anita Alvarez has been doing to this city and its people."[12]

THE STRUGGLE CONTINUES

Our work was never just about getting rid of elected officials. The system itself fails to meet the needs of all people. It was about exposing, once again, the systemic injustice Black people experience in

Chicago and sharing a vision to end it. BYP100 demands were clear, and to this day, with the exception of the demands since won, they haven't changed much:

- We demand all local, state, and federal budgets to defund the police and invest those dollars and resources in Black futures.
- We want reparations for chattel slavery, Jim Crow, and mass incarceration.
- We want to end all profit from so-called criminal justice punishment—both public and private.
- We want a guaranteed income for all, living wages, a federal jobs program, and freedom from discrimination for all workers.
- We want the labor of Black transgender and cisgender women (unseen and seen, unpaid and paid) to be valued and supported, not criminalized and marginalized.
- We want investments in Black communities that promote economic sustainability and eliminate the displacement of our people.

The story of why it was crucial to defeat Alvarez is connected to a long-standing tradition of systemic violence stemming from the institution of policing in the United States. Alvarez was a big player in the cover-up of the police killing of Laquan McDonald. She held the power to prosecute police officers who killed both Rekia Boyd and Laquan McDonald, and she consistently erred on the side of the CPD. The City of Chicago invests heavily in its police, in recent years allocating nearly 40 percent of its public service budget to the surveillance and control of Black and Brown communities across the city.[13] We are tied up in policing in more ways than one. The Chicago Police Department is one of the largest employers in the city, employing Black and Brown folks who invest in the institution of policing. The CPD is also one of the few agencies (or maybe the only one) that people believe can create conditions of safety—despite evidence that tells us otherwise. This institution didn't grow overnight, and it is deeply entwined with an international crew of morally inept people who cloak violence under the label of "public safety." While many proclaim that only a few cops are rotten apples, we must remember the second part of the phrase, that one bad apple spoils the bunch. And Chicago has a history of bad apples.

Community organizers are confronted with the dilemma of how to dismantle and build alternatives to policing that meet the material and emotional needs of our people. Imprisoning cops won't end policing or violence. Chicago organizers address that dilemma by building community to dream and scheme. But we've done so at great costs, including time, energy, and physical and financial resources. It costs money to pay for labor, printed materials, meeting space, food, websites, street teams, posters, art materials, and travel. The emotional, physical, and spiritual cost of putting our bodies and livelihoods on the line for justice has been high. While some relationships were built, others were broken in the process of movement building in Chicago. People hurt each other, and at times people took responsibility for their actions as a first step to repair the harm done.

I've learned that so much internal conflict emerges because people want their work and stories to been seen and valued. When that doesn't happen, especially in instances where the media is involved and aggravates already-present tensions, individuals and the broader movement both suffer. One television spot can spiral into a conflict that impacts the work and aggravates ongoing tensions.

Chicago's activists and community organizers are continuing the long struggle begun by our ancestors. Young and old, we have inherited a struggle that future generations will also take up. The stories I've shared here illustrate core components of the Chicago Model. First, the Chicago Model is intergenerational, with a strong history of community building. Second, it continues to be shaped through agitation and high-impact work by leaders from feminist and queer threads in the Black radical tradition. Third, Chicago organizing is historically local, national, and global. Last, it requires the involvement of multiple institutions with varying political alignment. The Chicago Model isn't applicable in every single context, but it is critical for movement strategists to study and learn from our movement history. Like any model, it is not a blueprint—the Chicago Model is a source of inspiration and vision for the challenges that emerge when people engage in mass movement work.

Movement building in Chicago means navigating a terrain of civil rights organizations, labor unions, street organizations, Black elected officials, wealthy Black families, immigrant communities, and faith-based institutions, including the Nation of Islam and Christian churches like Trinity United Church of Christ. We contend with multiple narratives, strategies, and tactics. The Chicago organizing community is not monolithic but includes strong bands of radical leaders who work within a broader progressive ecosystem, pushing and winning campaigns, advancing often unheard (and undervalued) narratives to create transformative change to improve the material conditions of our people's lives.

There is so much more that happened between 2014 and 2016 in Chicago's organizing community. The contributions outlined here reflect just a small percentage of the campaigns and efforts in Chicago organizing since the 1970s. The anti-eviction campaign mentioned above and the Dyett High School hunger strike are two of many that deserve further exploration. The role of the educators and students at Village Leadership Academy, who were pivotal in community organizing over the past several years, deserves more prominence in discussions about what it means to educate Black children who can lead movements. The Chicago arts community, including groups like Young Chicago Authors, Kuumba Lynx, and the Chicago Light

Brigade, continues to play a leading role in shaping movements. For people unfamiliar with this history, this book is meant as a starting point from which to construct a working model for organizing. It is meant not as an authoritative account but as an invitation for more organizers to tell their stories for the sake of informing our work toward collective liberation.

THE MANDATE

The mandate for Black people in this time is:

> *To avenge the suffering of our ancestors*
> *To earn the respect of future generations*
> *To be willing to be transformed in the service of the work.*

—MARY HOOKS,
codirector of Southerners on New Ground

This mandate, now recited across Black movement spaces, is an invitation. I am driven by the mandate as I sense Harriet Tubman at my back and hear Marsha P. Johnson telling me to "pay it no mind." The ancestors knew what was necessary while they lived, and they speak to us through the protest, art, and intellectual labor. As our elders emphasize, Black liberation is a long and protracted struggle. We have to be in this for the long haul. Even when we live in a world without prisons and policing (yes, I'm claiming it now, that one day we will), ongoing movement work will be needed to carry it ahead. Future generations will have the task of reimagining what must be done. They will push the growing edges of our movement, defend what works for them, and shed what doesn't. They will encounter predictable challenges and ones unforeseen.

The fiction of the United States of America allows independence to exist alongside slavery and freedom to exist alongside systemic sexual violence and a vast network of prisons. This fiction (or collection of lies) has conditioned our minds, violated our bodies, and allowed the squandering of the earth's resources for profit. This is the work of centuries of systemic violence in service of greed and control.

In the fiction of the United States, the founding "fathers" are liberators, not slavers and makers of genocide of Indigenous peoples. In the fiction of the United States there is one way to be human, one way to be a woman, and one way to be a man. One does not have autonomy over one's own body, and community self-determination is devalued and under constant attack.

Capitalism, patriarchy, anti-Blackness and white supremacy work together to destroy people and the land we depend on. We see this collusion in disaster after disaster—hurricanes due to climate change and floods where human-made infrastructure fails or exacerbates problems. We taste this collusion in highly processed food and we feel it as our paychecks increasingly fail to cover even basic needs. We see this collusion in extraction of land and exploitation of people. It is a great challenge, but we must continue to imagine—and work for—a world in which everyone is able to live with dignity and in right relationship with the land we inhabit.

The Black radical tradition exemplifies the struggle to break down the fictions and move toward dignity. Our tradition asserts that transformation is not only possible but also absolutely necessary for continued survival of all people and the planet. Our charge goes beyond the government. Our work today is about redefining humanity and transforming our relationships with each other and with the land.

There are still deep questions to answer and much work to be done. What claim do Black Americans have to the land Native peoples call Turtle Island? What claim to indigeneity? Our lineage goes back centuries to slavery and Africa and the Caribbean. Processes of colonization, forced migration, and enslavement have stripped us from our land, and we have always had to fight for it. It is anti-Black to say that after more than three hundred years of labor we have no claim to steward this land. Stewardship, not extractive ownership, should be our North Star. We should not and cannot allow the United States to set up shop on the continent of Africa without consent, as it has done, occupying lands, displacing and oppressing people who were already there. As descendants of enslaved and migrant people, our claim is not one of dominion but one of recognition and right to stewardship. We might, as comrades in Colombia have, go further and claim territory, in the midst of capitalist and state-sanctioned violence, in order to keep our people safe.

It is a fiction that the descendants of enslaved Africans don't have a justifiable claim to stewarding land in North America. The history of anti-Blackness and enslavement of Black people even within indigenous territories is not fiction. At the same time, there is also a history of Black people serving as agents of the US military to carry out its violence against Native peoples. We have to reckon with that history as well as that of slavery and understand that the majority of our people have lived and died under conditions of state-sanctioned terrorism. Our movement must foster transformative conversations among Black folks and Native peoples. Where are we supposed to live? We are not each other's enemies, and we should strive to aid each other's harvest in a world with too much scorched earth. The empire flourishes on our conflict. I believe that we are inherently stronger when we are together, moving in the same direction regardless of tactics.

Together we can imagine and move toward transformative change in our lifetimes and for future generations. Despite extraction from the earth, vast mining worldwide that continues to this day, there is still enough land on which to live and farm. We need to tend to the earth collectively, with a mind toward regeneration. Climate justice and labor movement organizations frame this as a "just transition." Movement Generation defines a just transition as an intentional pathway that moves us "towards local, living, loving economies."

This will not happen without retaliation and repression from the state and corporations. A just transition will not serve the interests of the greedy, domineering profiteers. It will serve the collective liberation of all people. The alternative to committing to that—and all the work it entails—is the complete degradation of Earth and everything that lives on it. Let us build now what we want and what we need. If we ever reach out into the depths of the galaxy beyond Earth—as Afro-futurists imagine—we have to be prepared.

I have devoted few words to white people in this book, much less white women. If the 2016 presidential election, the pivotal 2017 Virginia gubernatorial election, and the 2017 Alabama senate election demonstrate anything—over 50 percent of white women voters voted for the Republican candidate in each—it is the unreliability of white women to vote with the interests of marginalized communities. Black women on the other hand, consistently show up for the Democratic Party, even when it does not invest in Black people or our communities despite having the ability to do so. White liberals and progressives hold too much control over political institutions, resources, and policy—and consequently too much power over our very lives. That power should be relinquished. It's been held for far too long and deployed against the interests of Black people and a myriad of other marginalized people. For white folks who want to be a part of transforming the world, follow the lead of today's movement for Black lives. No single leader is coming to save us. Only collective action can bring about the transformation our world needs.

Our movement must build institutions, organizations, practices, and a movement culture that future generations can respect and love enough to continue while challenging the imperfections. A single person cannot lead a successful movement. Each of us has a role in the work of movement building and must assume that responsibility. As we amass freedoms and experience collective liberation, which I believe is possible, we cannot recycle the master's tools, systems, or thinking. The movement must commit to leadership development, healing justice, and combating liberalism through principled struggle. Community organizers and activists must interrogate who we are as individuals, who our people are, and what we are building, and we must ask if we are actually ready to win. Chicago's legacies of resistance and movement building are at the forefront of this thinking. It is my hope that Chicago can serve as one model among many to guide movement building work.

Our collective struggle as Black people is both transnational and local, around the globe and within our hearts. The ongoing project of colonialism lives in each of us and manifests itself in our movement. It shows up in the promotion of disaster capitalism in response to rebuilding Puerto Rico and the US Virgin Islands. It shows up in trials by social media and in the inadequacy of movement institutions to address structural violence and trauma. Therefore, we must take up the work of decolonization, the process of dismantling governmental and cultural systems that control and strip nations, peoples, and groups of self-determination and sovereignty. Independence movements across the Southern Hemisphere may be the most obvious examples of decolonization, but the process doesn't end at a declaration of independence. Breaking down what has been learned under colonialism, eradicating internalized colonialism, and disrupting and displacing those who continue to benefit from it—these projects remain long after Independence Day.

Our collective imaginations must burst open in order to believe that liberation is possible. People have to feel the possibility of liberation. History and today's movement teach us that Black folks have held the line of resistance for centuries. Resistance is not new, yet today's realities require the movement to push its growing edges, tell more complete stories, and construct more complete solutions. Colonization affects what people think and do. From the days of extermination campaigns and the forced removal of Native peoples to rural and urban economically depressed communities, the US empire has been run by corporate interests and based upon state-sanctioned violence. Still, people resist. In taking decolonization into our work, we do not ignore the need to dismantle white supremacy, patriarchy, and capitalism. We see a bigger picture, one including all oppressed peoples. We believe in the real possibility of abolition and building a better world. We believe that an economy that is generative, not extractive, is possible and necessary.

This is a call to celebrate the inherent value of all Black people. It is a call to queer our movement practices and honor the contributions of Black feminist and LGBTQ movements to the Black radical tradition. And it is a mandate to organize. In doing so, we can make the world the place we want it to be, liberate ourselves from oppression, and create social, cultural, and political systems that are liberatory and just for all. Our movement can and will hold each of these elements, and we must succeed for the sake of collective liberation.

ACKNOWLEDGMENTS

This book is possible because of so many people who contributed their energy to my life and to the long-term struggle for Black liberation. I am deeply grateful for my family, my comrades, and the people who drive me to meet my commitments to myself and our movement.

I am thankful for the team at Beacon Press, including my editor Gayatri Patnaik, for her honesty and guidance. I am grateful to Jill Petty, just as much of a doula to this book as anyone else is, for sending me a LinkedIn message and saying yes to lunch that led me to Beacon. You and Beacon took a chance on a first-time author, and I am forever grateful for that. To my literary agent, Tanya McKinnon, thank you for challenging me to bring my full self into this book.

Thanks to my political home, BYP100. Our members and my colleagues gave me the space, inspiration, and motivation to finish this book. Thank you, Fresco (our minister of culture), Asha (thank you for introducing me to prison abolition), Tasha, Brianna, L'lerret, Aaron, Sam, Nzinga, and Rebba. It's been almost five years, team, and our community has sharpened me beyond measure and shown me what it means to truly love our people. As I transition from my role at BYP100 to the next phase of my work for Black liberation, know that I remain committed to our vision, mission, and core values.

Thank you to Rose S. Afriyie, for reading parts of the manuscript and being a loyal sister friend. You always have my front and my back.

Thank you to Alexis Pegues for answering my panicked calls about any given life crisis and always handling me with care.

Comrade, sister, and friend Janae Bonsu, you read this book before anyone else did and cared enough to make the first rounds of edits. I owe you more than I can ever repay.

Patricia Jerido, you are more than a life coach—you have saved my life over and over again. To the teachers at Black Organizing for Leadership and Dignity (BOLD), thank you for creating a vehicle for my personal transformation and the transformation of our movement. I bow in gratitude to each of you.

Thank you to the OGs whose advice and examples are constantly swimming in my mind: Kai Lumumba, Makani Themba, Denise Perry, Barbara Smith and the Combahee River Collective, Beverly Guy Sheftall, Mariame Kaba, Beth E. Richie, and Coach Brenda Harris. Cathy J. Cohen, who knew that a coffee at Z&H in Hyde Park would lead us to where we are now? You are my scholar, activist, and Black lesbian possibility model! Barbara Ransby, thank you for sharing your genius, family, and wisdom with me. Neither BYP100 nor I would be as sharp as we are without you.

My development as a leader and as a person would not be possible without the many relationships I've formed over the years. Thank you to Martin Trimble and Kathleen O'Toole for teaching me good habits as a very young organizer. Thanks to comrades in the Chicago organizing community and the Movement for Black Lives. Chicago, the world is watching us because we are a site of resistance and love for our people. The struggle continues through each of you.

I wouldn't have a clear view of the world were it not for Professor William Munro leading my first trip to South Africa. Thank you to Ahmad Abuznaid for remembering that conversation we had in Miami about Palestine.

I wrote most of this book in coffee shops across Chicago and New York City. Thank you to the kind and generous people working at the

Currency Exchange Café. Megan, Chrissy, Sydney, and everyone else there were often the first people I saw during my early-morning writing sessions. Thank you to the Social Change Initiative team for the 2017 fellowship experience and for providing me with the resources I needed to finish this book.

Black women have saved my life over and over, and I am forever indebted to so many. Thank you to those who I interviewed for this project, including Ash-Lee Henderson, Elle Hearns, Dara Cooper, and Rukia Lumumba. Thank you to Neichelle Guidry for being a writing buddy. I am thankful for our ancestors Marsha P. Johnson, Rosa Parks, Recy Taylor, Ella Baker, Gwendolyn Brooks, and Fannie Lou Hamer for lighting the way. Thank you to the BlackOut Collective, especially Celeste, Chinyere, and Karissa for embodying beautiful disruption. N'Tanya Lee for helping me to crystallize what principled struggle can look like. Alsie Parks, thank you for answering the call when I needed help researching the depth of topics explored in this book. And adrienne maree brown, thank you for holding our team and me through tough and beautiful moments.

Special thanks to Ai-Jen Poo, Deepa Iyer, and Luvvie Ajayi for helping me figure out the book-writing process. Thank you to Samantha Master and JeNae Taylor for being ears and shoulders to lean on. Thank you to my friend and comrade Kai M. Green for your enduring support, trusting me with your students, and sharing my work with your colleagues at Williams College. Gratitude to Movement Generation comrades for blowing my mind. Thanks to Becky Belcore and the NAKASEC team for your commitment to Black liberation.

Mary Hooks, my comrade and partner in life, thank you for being a vessel for our ancestors and for loving me. Thank you for allowing our ancestors to use you as a medium to give our people the mandate.

I bow in deep deference to my ancestors for being at my back and reminding me that change is not only possible, it is inevitable.

Lastly, I am deeply thankful to my parents, Charles and Gwen, for bringing me into this world and always encouraging me to go as far as my mind could fathom. You raised me, and you raised Charlita, Charles, and Sarai. Thank you.

NOTES

CHAPTER 1: ALL OF US OR NONE OF US

1. Bill Allison, Mira Rojanasakul, Brittany Harris, and Cedric Sam, "Tracking the 2016 Presidential Money Race," *Bloomberg*, December 9, 2016, https://www.bloomberg.com/politics/graphics/2016-presidential-campaign-fundraising.

2. John Judis, "Why Identity Politics Couldn't Clinch a Clinton Win," *Washington Post*, November 11, 2016.

3. Mark Lilla, "The End of Identity Liberalism," *New York Times*, November 18, 2016.

4. Judis, "Why Identity Politics Couldn't Clinch a Clinton Win."

5. Combahee River Collective, *Combahee River Collective Statement: Black Feminist Organizing in the Seventies and Eighties* (New York: Kitchen Table/Women of Color Press, 1986).

6. Beverly Guy-Sheftall, ed., *Words of Fire: An Anthology of African American Feminist Thought* (New York: New Press, 2011).

7. Cathy J. Cohen, "Punks, Bulldaggers, and Welfare Queens: The Radical Potential of Queer Politics?" *GLQ* 3 (1997): 437–65.

8. "Community and Organization Accountability Process Update," *Transforming Harm*, http://transformharm.tumblr.com/post/140296664386/community-and-organization-accountability-process.

CHAPTER 2: REVIVING THE BLACK RADICAL IMAGINATION

1. Jana Winter and Sharon Weinberger, "The FBI's New US Terrorist Threat: 'Black Identity Extremists,'" *Foreign Policy*, October 6, 2017, http://foreignpolicy.com/2017/10/06/the-fbi-has-identified-a-new-domestic-terrorist-threat-and-its-black-identity-extremists.

2. Rebecca Onion, "Interactive Map Catalogs a History of Collective Violence Against Black Communities," *Slate*, July 6, 2015, www.slate.com/blogs/the_vault/2015/07/06/history_of_violence_against_black_communities_mapping_project_for_lynching.html.

3. Beth E. Richie, *Arrested Justice: Black Women, Violence, and America's Prison Nation* (New York: New York University Press, 2012), 133.

4. Scott Nagawa, "Blackness Is the Fulcrum," *Race Files*, May 4, 2002, https://www.racefiles.com/2012/05/04/blackness-is-the-fulcrum.

5. Ella Baker, "The Black Woman in the Civil Rights Struggle," speech given at the Black World Conference, Atlanta, 1969.

6. "Cicely Tyson Looks Back at Acting Career, Life," CBS News, December 16, 2015, https://www.cbsnews.com/news/cicely-tyson-acting -modeling-pioneer-african-american-women-kennedy-center-honor.

CHAPTER 3: A CASE FOR REIMAGINING THE BLACK RADICAL TRADITION

1. Danielle McGuire, *At the Dark End of the Street: Black Women, Rape and Resistance: A New History of the Civil Rights Movement from Rosa Parks to the Rise of Black Power* (New York: Vintage, 2010).

2. Ibid., 37.

3. Ibid., 29.

4. Kimberly Springer, *Living for the Revolution, Black Feminist Organizations, 1968–1980* (Durham, NC: Duke University Press, 2005), 2.

5. Joy James, *Seeking the Beloved Community: A Feminist Race Reader* (Albany: SUNY Press, 2014), 41.

6. Thomas Sankara, *Thomas Sankara Speaks* (New York: Pathfinder Press, 2007).

7. "When they confront race and gender stereotypes, black women are standing in a crooked room, and they have to figure out which way is up." Melissa Harris-Perry, *Sister Citizen: Shame Stereotypes and Black Women in America* (New Haven, CT: Yale University Press, 2011).

8. The Compton's Cafeteria riot took place in the Tenderloin District of San Francisco in August 1966 after a drag queen was physically assaulted by a police officer. Compton's was one of the few places where transgender and queer people, drag queens, entertainers, and people who did sex work could gather safely.

CHAPTER 4: THREE COMMITMENTS

1. Melissa Harris-Perry, "How #SquadCare Saved My Life," *Elle*, July 24, 2017, http://www.elle.com/culture/career-politics/news/a46797/squad-care -melissa-harris-perry.

2. Black Emotional and Mental Health Collective, http://www.beam .community/healing-justice/.

3. Ibid.

4. Leah Lakshmi Piepzna-Samarasinha, "A Not-So-Brief Personal History of the Healing Justice Movement, 2010–2016," *Mice Magazine* (Fall 2016), http://micemagazine.ca/.

5. As a leader, Mao was not without contradictions. Though his political thought served as a beacon of what a class-based struggle could look like outside a European context, he would go on to lead a revolution that involved death and devastation to millions.

6. Robin D. G. Kelley, "Black Like Mao," *Souls: A Critical Journal of Black Politics Culture and Society* 1, no. 4 (Fall 1999).

7. Mao Tse-Tung, "Combat Liberalism," September 9, 1937, Marxists Internet Archive, https://www.marxists.org/reference/archive/mao/selected -works/volume-2/mswv2_03.htm.

CHAPTER 5: FIVE QUESTIONS

1. "Reproductive justice" means ensuring the rights to maintain personal bodily autonomy, have children or not have children, and parent the children we have in safe and sustainable communities.

2. Barbara Ransby, "Quilting a Movement," *In These Times*, April 4, 2011.

3. "What Is the PIC? What Is Abolition?," Critical Resistance, http://criticalresistance.org/about/not-so-common-language.

4. Ibid.

5. BYP100, Law for Black Lives, Center for Popular Democracy, *Freedom to Thrive: Reimagining Safety & Security in Our Communities* (2017) http://populardemocracy.org/sites/default/files/Freedom%20To%20Thrive %2C%20Higher%20Res%20Version.pdf.

CHAPTER 6: THE CHICAGO MODEL

1. Ethan Michaeli, "Bound for the Promised Land," *Atlantic*, January 11, 2016, https://www.theatlantic.com/politics/archive/2016/01/chicago -defender/422583.

2. Richard Wright's line is also the title of Isabel Wilkerson's *The Warmth of Other Suns: The Epic Story of America's Great Migration* (New York: Random House, 2010).

3. Michael C. Dawson, *Blacks in and out of the Left* (Cambridge, MA: Harvard University Press, 2013).

4. Darlene Clark Hine, *Hine Sight: Black Women and the Re-Construction of American History* (Bloomington: Indiana University Press, 1998), 98.

5. International Association of Chiefs of Police, *FY 2011–2016 Strategic Plan*, www.theiacp.org/portals/0/pdfs/IACPStrategicPlan.pdf.

6. Allison Flowers, "Chicago's Torture Victims Want Justice," *Vice*, September 22, 2014, https://www.vice.com/en_us/article/xd5753/the -chicago-police-departments-torture-victims-want-justice-0000431 -v21n9.

7. Araz Hachadourian, "Chicago Just Became the First US City to Pay Reparations to Victims of Police Torture," *Yes Magazine*, May 15, 2015, http://www.yesmagazine.org/peace-justice/chicago-is-the-first-city-to-offer -reparations-for-victims-of-police-violence-now-they-want-to-make-sure-no -one-forgets.

8. N'COBRA, National Coalition of Blacks for Reparations in America, www.ncobraonline.org/about-ncobra.

9. Chicago Torture Justice Memorials, http://chicagotorture.org/project.

10. Ibid.

11. Jenn Jackson, "A Discussion with Mariame Kaba on the #ByeAnita Campaign and Grassroots Organizing," Black Youth Project Blog, November 29, 2016, http://blackyouthproject.com/a-discussion-with-mariame -kaba-on-the-byeanita-campaign-and-grassroots-organizing.

12. Leah Hope and Laura Thoren, "Kim Foxx Defeats Anita Alvarez in Cook County State's Attorney Primary," ABC 7 News, March 16, 2016, http://abc7chicago.com/politics/foxx-defeats-alvarez-in-cook-county-states -attorney-primary/1247992.

13. "2017 City of Chicago Budget Ordinance," City of Chicago, https:// www.cityofchicago.org/content/dam/city/depts/obm/supp_info/2017%20 Budget/2017BudgetOrdinance.pdf.

INDEX

abolition, use of term, x. *See also* systemic/structural change
Abu-Jamal, Mumia, 72
Abuznaid, Ahmad, 29
accountability/accepting responsibility: community accountability, 98; and effectiveness, 12–13, 16, 41; and liberalism, 80, 82, 84; principled struggle, 78–79, 81–84; and transformative justice processes, xi, 15–18, 76; willingness to govern, 108–9. *See also* healing justice; leadership; sexual violence
Action Now, 126, 128
activists/activism. *See* community organizing; organizers and activists
activist traditions. *See* Black radical tradition; education, political
Affordable Care Act ("Obamacare"), 21
Africa: the African slave trade, 36; capitalist incursions, 137; trip to Ghana, 28–29. *See also* anti-Blackness; slavery
Afriyie, Rose, xvi, 14, 64
Afro-Palestinians, collective punishment of, 31
Alabama Brotherhood of Sleeping Car Porters, 47

Alabama Committee for Equal Justice for Mrs. Recy Taylor, 46–48
Alhassen, Maytha, 29
Alim, Troy, 128
Alinsky, Saul, 9, 94
Alvarez, Anita: and the Boyd killing, 131; campaign to oust, 125–26, 130; election defeat, 130; and the McDonald killing, 126–27, 131
Amnesty International USA, 122
angst/anxiety, collective: and decision-making, 102–3; personal, recognizing and sharing, 95, 100
anti-Blackness: and collective punishment, 29, 31; entrenchment of, 21; and gendered violence, 33–34; global scope, xiv–xv, 25–26; internalizing, 26, 36, 100–101; links with capitalism, patriarchy, white supremacy, xv, 33, 136; and mass criminalization/violence, 27–28, 30–31, 102–3, 117–18; and power relationships, 55, 105; and strategy of division, 96–99; use of term, x; viewing Blacks as a monolith, 57; viewing Blacks as slaves-in-waiting, 26. *See*